ACTION RESEARCH:

A GUIDE FOR THE
TEACHER RESEARCHER

GEOFFREY E. MILLS
Southern Oregon University

Merrill, an imprint of Prentice Hall
Upper Saddle River, New Jersey • *Columbus, Ohio*

Library of Congress Cataloging-in-Publication Data

Mills, Geoffrey E.
    Action research : a guide for the teacher researcher / Geoffrey E.
Mills.
       p.   cm.
    Includes bibliographical references (p.) and index.
    ISBN 0-13-772047-5
    1. Action research in education—United States—Handbooks,
manuals, etc.   2. Teaching—United States—Handbooks, manuals, etc.
I. Title.
LB1028.24.M55   2000
370' .7—dc21   98-55963
                                                      CIP

Cover photo: Uniphoto
Executive Editor: Kevin M. Davis
Developmental Editor: Gianna Marsella
Production Editor: Julie Peters
Editorial Assistant: Holly Jennings
Design Coordinator: Diane C. Lorenzo
Cover Designer: Rod Harris
Production Manager: Laura M. Messerly
Director of Marketing: Kevin Flanagan
Marketing Manager: Meghan McCauley
Marketing Coordinator: Krista Groshong

This book was set in Garamond by The Clarinda Company and was printed and bound by
R.R. Donnelley & Sons Company. The cover was printed by Phoenix Color Corp.

©2000 by Prentice-Hall, Inc.
Pearson Education
Upper Saddle River, New Jersey 07458

Printed in the United States of America

10 9 8 7 6 5 4 3 2 1

ISBN: 0-13-772047-5

Prentice-Hall International (UK) Limited, *London*
Prentice-Hall of Australia Pty. Limited, *Sydney*
Prentice-Hall of Canada, Inc., *Toronto*
Prentice-Hall Hispanoamericana, S. A., *Mexico*
Prentice-Hall of India Private Limited, *New Delhi*
Prentice-Hall of Japan, Inc., *Tokyo*
Prentice-Hall (Singapore) Pte. Ltd., *Singapore*
Editora Prentice-Hall do Brasil, Ltda., *Rio de Janeiro*

For Audrey Mills, Dr. Milton H. Brown and Catherine S. Brown—
Your love, support and spirit live with me always.

Preface

The Role of Action Research in Effecting Educational Change

Action research has the potential to be a powerful agent of educational change. Action research helps to develop teachers and administrators with professional attitudes that embrace action, progress, and reform rather than stability and mediocrity. In addition, the action research process fosters a democratic approach to decision making while, at the same time it empowers individual teachers through participation in a collaborative, socially responsive research activity.

Commitment to action research positions teachers and administrators as learners rather than experts. Those committed to action research will willingly undertake continued professional development because they believe that there is a gap between the real worlds of their daily teaching practices and their vision of an ideal one.

Incorporating action research into preservice teacher education programs and professional development programs for inservice teachers will help make action research an ongoing component of a professional teacher's practice. Such action will ultimately help teachers to incorporate action research alongside other critical components of teaching, such as curriculum development, authentic assessment strategies, classroom management strategies, teaching strategies, and caring for children. Such actions will encourage teachers to embrace change.

It is my hope that this book will, in some small part, help us all to move forward, to struggle ahead in the face of difficult times. Action research is an invitation to learn, a means to tackle tough questions that face us individually and collectively as teachers, and a method for questioning our daily taken-for-granted assumptions as a way to find hope for the future.

Conceptual Framework and Organization of the Text

This book has emerged over a number of years based on my experience of doing and teaching action research. During this time I have had the opportunity to work with some outstanding teachers and principals who were committed to looking systematically at the effects of their programs on the lives of children. This book's organization has grown out of these experiences and has been field tested by numerous students and colleagues.

Each chapter opens with an action research vignette that illustrates the content that will follow. These vignettes, most of which have been written by teachers and principals with whom I have worked, show readers who does action research and what action research looks like in practice. The order of these chapters roughly matches the action research process, an approach that I have found very successful when teaching action research.

The first chapter defines action research and provides historical and theoretical contexts for the rest of the book. The first chapter also reviews various models of action research and concludes with the four-step process: identifying an area of focus, collecting data, analyzing and interpreting data, and action planning, and the dialectic model that this book is based on. The remaining chapters mirror these steps.

Chapter 2 helps action researchers choose an "area of focus." Guidelines for selecting an area of focus are offered along with step-by-step directions for how to do a literature review using on-line resources such as ERIC. The chapter culminates with an action research plan that provides a practical guide for moving teacher researchers through the action research process.

Chapter 3 offers a comprehensive discussion on qualitative data collection that covers the "3 Es" of data collection: experiencing, enquiring, and examining.

Chapter 4 addresses important data collection considerations such as validity, reliability, and generalizability to ensure that the data collected will be "trustworthy." The chapter also offers ethical guideposts and poses an ethical dilemma vignette to spark teacher researchers' thinking about how best to resolve ethical dilemmas if, and when, they arise.

Chapter 5 describes selected techniques of data analysis and data interpretation and distinguishes between the goals of the two processes.

Chapter 6 helps teacher researchers take action using a helpful Steps to Action Chart. The chapter also discusses the potential obstacles to change that teacher researchers might face and suggests strategies for overcoming these obstacles.

Chapter 7 discusses the importance of bridging the gap between research and practice and following through with the complete action research cycle to ensure that the findings of the research have an impact on student learning. The importance of sharing, critiquing, and celebrating action research is also covered.

Chapter 8 provides guidelines for using the action research resources offered on the Internet, including action research web sites, listservs, and on-line journals.

Finally, chapter 9 provides an extended example of action research through a case study of Curtis Elementary. The case study follows the process described throughout the book and includes an evaluation of the project on the basis of criteria for judging the quality of action research.

Features of the Text

The text's user-friendly format includes chapter objectives, key concepts boxes, research in action checklists, chapter summaries, and questions for further thought. The text also includes many practical illustrations of the action research process that will help teacher researchers apply the process in their own school or classroom setting. The unique chapter 8, which provides on-line action research resources, will be a welcome feature to teacher researchers who wish to interact with other action researchers and access the plethora of action research resources available on the Internet.

Acknowledgments

I would like to thank the many reviewers of this manuscript provided by the editorial staff at Merrill/Prentice Hall who invested a great deal of time and provided critical feedback during the development of this book. These reviewers include Robert Fallows, Northern Arizona University, Tucson; Gonzalo Garcia, Jr., Texas A & M University; Samuel L. Guskin, Indiana University, Bloomington; L. Riley Hodges, City University; Ochieng' K'Olewe, Western Maryland University; Gail McCutcheon, The Ohio State University; and Teresa Prosser, Webster University.

I would also like to acknowledge the staff at Merrill/Prentice Hall without whose guidance (and patience!) this book would not have become a reality. In particular, I would like to thank Kevin Davis, Executive Editor, for his decision to work with me to develop a practical action research guide for teachers; Gianna Marsella, Developmental Editor, who continually frightened me with emails saying, "I had a great idea over the weekend!" and who taught me how to think about my writing in new and creative ways; and Cindy Peck, copy editor, for her outstanding word-smithing skills.

I would also like to extend my gratitude to the hundreds of students at Southern Oregon University who responded to various drafts of this book and also endured my ramblings about learning how to write. Their insights into what makes a text user friendly have been greatly appreciated and are reflected in the text. Similarly, I have had the pleasure of working with hundreds of teachers throughout Oregon who taught me what needed to be included in a "helpful" book.

Close colleagues and co-action researchers also provided valuable feedback. These individuals include Tom Schram (University of New Hampshire); Marty Turner (Southern Oregon University); Steve Boyarsky (Jackson Educational Service District); Cheri Page (Roseburg Public Schools, Oregon); Mary-Curtis Gramley (Southern Oregon University); Joe Senese, Lauren Fagel, Paul Swanson, and John Gorleski (Highland Park High School, Illinois); and Donna Mills (Southern Oregon University). I am indebted to the time they have committed to reading and responding to drafts of the manuscript.

I would also like to thank my friend and mentor, Harry Wolcott (University of Oregon), for his encouragement and insights throughout the writing process.

Finally, I would like to acknowledge the support and encouragement of my wife, colleague, and best friend, Donna Mills, who endured my mood swings and weekend writing commitments throughout this lengthy process. And I would like to thank my son Jonathan, who gave up play time with his dad and continually reminded me of three important things: (1) what it means to be a teacher and a learner, (2) that I must exercise every day so that I keep up with his energy and enthusiasm for life, and (3) that it's always the computer's fault when things don't work the way they are meant to!

Geoff Mills

Brief Contents

Contents

CHAPTER 1

Understanding Action Research

This chapter introduces the topic of action research by providing an example of an action research project from a real teacher-researcher, an exploration of the historical and theoretical foundations of action research, a discussion of the goals and justification for action research, and an explanation of the action research process.

―――

After reading this chapter you should be able to

1. Define action research.
2. Describe the historical foundations of action research.
3. Identify the similarities and differences between critical/postmodern and practical theories of action research.
4. Describe the goals of and justification for action research.
5. List the four stages of the action research process.

What Motivates Unmotivated Students?
DEBORAH SOUTH

Deborah South, a high school teacher in a rural Oregon high school, was a participant in an action research class. She shares the challenges she faced when, due to a last-minute teaching assignment, she found herself working with a group of "unmotivated" students. Deborah's story illustrates the wide variety of factors that can influence students' learning and a teacher's willingness to look critically at her teaching methods and how they affected the children in her classroom. While Deborah's interpretation of the results of her study did not validate her practice, it did provide data that Deborah and the school's principal could use to make changes to the existing curriculum for "unmotivated" students.

Teaching students who are unmotivated and apathetic can be a difficult challenge for any teacher to overcome. These students typically can be disruptive and negative and often require an extraordinary amount of teacher time to manage the students' behavior. My concern with teaching unmotivated students has existed almost since I began teaching five years ago. As an educator one tries all kinds of possible strategies to encourage students to be successful. With unmotivated students who are apathetic and exhibit unacceptable behavior, these strategies do not work. Eventually the patience runs out, and as ashamed as I am to admit it, I stop trying to find ways to reach these particular students. It soon becomes enough that they stay in their seats, be quiet, and do not disturb anyone.

However, last term my attitude was forced to change. I was given a study skills group of twenty of the lowest achieving eighth graders in the school. This new class consisted of sixteen boys and four girls. My task was to somehow take these students and miraculously make them motivated, achieving students. I was trained in a study skills program before the term started and thought that I was set to go: I had the students, I

had the curriculum, and I had the help of an outstanding aide.

Within a week, I sensed we were in trouble. My twenty students often showed up with no supplies. Their behavior was atrocious. They called each other names, threw various items around the room, and walked around the classroom when they felt like it. Their attitudes toward me were negative. I became concerned about teaching these students. Partly, I felt bad that they were so disillusioned with school and their future; partly, I felt bad because the thought of teaching in this environment every day for another fourteen weeks made me wish summer vacation were here.

Given this situation, I decided to do some reading about how other teachers motivate unmotivated students and to formulate some ideas about the variables that contribute to a student's success in school. Variables I investigated included adult approval, peer influence, and success in math, science, language arts, and social studies, as well as self-esteem and students' views of their academic abilities.

The majority of the data I collected was through surveys, interviews, and report card/attendance records in an effort to answer the following questions:

- How does attendance affect student performance?
- How are students influenced by their friends in completing schoolwork?
- How do adults (parents, teachers) affect the success of students?
- What levels of self-esteem do these students have?

As a result of this investigation, I learned many things. For example, for this group of students attendance does not appear to be a factor—with the exception of one student, they all come to school regularly. Not surprisingly, peer groups did affect student performance. Seventy-three percent of my students reported that their friends never encouraged doing homework or putting any effort into homework.

Another surprising result was the lack of impact of a teacher's approval on student achievement. Ninety-four percent of my students indicated that they never or seldom do their homework to receive teacher approval. Alternatively, 57 percent indicated that they often or always do their homework so that their families will be proud of them.

One of the most interesting things that arose during this study was the realization that most of my students misbehave out of frustration at their own lack of abilities. They are not being obnoxious to gain attention, but to draw attention away from the fact that they do not know how to complete the assigned work.

When I looked at report cards and compared grades over three quarters, I noticed a trend. Between the first and second quarter, student performance had increased. That is, most students were doing better than they had during the first quarter. Between the second and third quar-

ters, however, grades dropped dramatically. I tried to determine why that drop would occur, and the only common experience shared by these twenty students was the fact that they had been moved into my class at the beginning of the third quarter.

When I presented my project to the class during our end-of-term "celebration," I was convinced that the "cause" of the students' unmotivated behavior was my teaching. I had concluded through my data analysis and interpretation that the one experience these eighteen children had in common was participation in my study skills class. This conclusion, however, was not readily accepted by my critical friends and colleagues in the class who urged me to consider other interpretations of the data. For example, maybe the critical mass of negativity present in one classroom provided the children with a catalyst to act out against the teacher. After all, this was the only class shared exclusively by these twenty students. Afterward, I shared the findings of my study with my school principal. As a result, she decided not to group these students together homogeneously for a study skills class the following year.

■■
■■

A S YOU CAN SEE, action research is a "wonderfully uncomfortable" (Lytle, 1997) place to be—once we start our journey of investigation there is no way of knowing in advance where we will end up. Action research, like any other problem-solving process, is an ongoing creative activity that exposes us to surprises along the way. What appeared to matter in the planning stages of an action research investigation may provide us with only a hint, a scratching of the surface, of what is *really* the focus for our investigations. How we deal with the uncertainty of the journey positions us as learners of our own craft, an attitude that is critical to our success. This book attempts to foster an openness to the spirit of inquiry guided by action research.

A Brief Overview of Educational Research

When you hear the words *scientific research,* you probably think of a scientist in a white lab coat (usually a balding, middle-aged man with a pocket full of pens in his jacket!) mixing chemicals or doing experiments on white mice. Traditional scientists, like the one pictured in this rather trite image, proceed with their research under the assumption that "all behaviors and events are orderly" and that all events "have discoverable causes" (Gay, 1996, pp. 5–6.) This traditional belief that natural phenomena can be explained in an orderly way using empirical sciences is sometimes called **positivism**.

Human beings, however, are very complicated organisms, and compared to chemicals—and mice, for that matter—their behavior is disorderly and fairly unpredictable. This presents a challenge to educational researchers who are concerned with gaining insight into human behavior in educational environments such as schools and classrooms.

The goal of traditional educational research is "to explain, predict, and/or control educational phenomena" (Gay, 1996, p. 6). To do this, researchers try to manipulate and control certain **variables** (the factors that might affect the outcomes of a particular study) to test a **hypothesis** (a statement the researcher makes that predicts what will happen or explains what the outcome of the study will be).

For example, a researcher may be interested in studying the effects of a certain phonics program (the variable) on the rate at which children learn to read. The researcher may hypothesize that the use of this phonics program will shorten the time it takes for students to learn to read. To confirm or reject this hypothesis, he or she might study the reading progress of one group of children who were taught using the phonics program (the **experimental group**) and compare it to the reading progress of another group of children (called the **control group**) who were taught reading without the phonics program. Children would be **randomly** assigned to either the experimental or the control group as a way to reduce the differences that might exist in naturally occurring groups. At the end of the **experiment**, the researcher would compare the progress of each group and decide whether the hypothesis could be accepted or rejected with a predetermined level of **statistical significance** (for example, that the difference between the mean for the control group and the mean for the experimental group is large in comparison to the standard error). Finally, the researcher would present the findings of the study at a conference and perhaps publish the results.

This process may sound very straightforward. In classroom and school settings, however, it is difficult to control all of the factors that affect the outcomes of our teaching without disrupting our natural classroom environments. For example, how do we know that the phonics program is the *only* variable affecting the rate at which students learn to read? Perhaps some students are being read to at home by their parents; perhaps one teacher is more effective than another; perhaps one group of students gets to read more exciting books than the other; perhaps one group of children has difficulty concentrating on their reading because they all skipped breakfast!

Action researchers acknowledge and embrace these complications rather than trying to control them. In addition, action researchers differ from traditional researchers because they are committed to *taking action* and *effecting positive educational change* based on their findings rather than being satisfied with reporting their conclusions to others. Another difference is that while educational research has historically been done by university professors, scholars, and graduate students on children, teachers, and principals, action researchers are often the schoolteachers and principals who were formerly the subjects of educational research. As such, they participate in their *own* inquiries, acting as both teacher and researcher at the same time.

Finally, research is also categorized by the methods the researchers use. Simply put, different research problems require different research approaches. These approaches to educational research are often classified as either quantitative or qualitative research. **Quantitative research** focuses on controlling a small number of variables to determine cause-effect relationships and/or the strength of those relationships. This type of research uses numbers to quantify the cause-effect relationship. **Qualitative research** uses narrative, descriptive approaches to data collection to understand the way things are and what it means. Qualitative approaches might include, for example, conducting face-to-face interviews, making observations, and recording interactions on videotape. Key Concepts Box 1-1 compares traditional research and action research.

Although different, the two approaches need not be considered mutually exclusive; a given study might incorporate both quantitative *and* qualitative techniques. For example, a researcher interested in the relationship between student achievement and self-esteem might start her inquiry by comparing the grade point averages of high school students with their numerical scores on a multiple-choice questionnaire designed to measure their self-esteem. To gain a broader under-

KEY CONCEPTS BOX 1-1

A Comparison of Traditional Research and Action Research		
WHAT?	**TRADITIONAL RESEARCH**	**ACTION RESEARCH**
Who?	Conducted by university professors, scholars, and graduate students on experimental and control groups.	Conducted by teachers and principals on children in their care.
Where?	In environments where variables can be controlled.	In schools and classrooms.
How?	Using quantitative methods to show, to some predetermined degree of statistical significance, a cause-effect relationship between variables.	Using qualitative methods to describe what's happening and to understand the effects of some educational intervention.
Why?	To report and publish conclusions that can be generalized to larger populations.	To take action and effect positive educational change in the specific school environment that was studied.

standing of this complicated relationship, the researcher might also interview and observe a number of students to gather additional data.

The area of focus or **research question** identified by the researcher will determine the most appropriate approach (quantitative and/or qualitative) to use. Because most action researchers use narrative, descriptive methods, the emphasis in this book will be on the use of qualitative research.

Defining Action Research

Over the past decade, the typical "required" research course in many schools of teacher education has changed from a traditional survey class on research methods to a more practical research course that either focuses on or includes the topic of action research. But what is action research, and why is it capturing the attention of teachers and administrators?

Action research is any systematic inquiry conducted by teacher researchers, principals, school counselors, or other stakeholders in the teaching/learning environment, to gather information about the ways that their particular schools operate, how they teach, and how well their students learn. This information is gathered with the goals of gaining insight, developing reflective practice, effecting positive changes in the school environment (and on educational practices in general), and improving student outcomes and the lives of those involved.

Action research is research done *by* teachers, *for* themselves; it is not imposed on them by someone else. Action research engages teachers in a four-step process, namely to

1. Identify an area of focus.
2. Collect data.
3. Analyze and interpret data.
4. Develop an action plan.

Before we elaborate on these four steps, however, we will explore the historical antecedents of action research and the theoretical foundations of current action research practices. As you read these descriptions, consider which philosophy best fits your beliefs about action research, teaching, and learning. Then begin to consider how you might incorporate action research into your professional life.

Origins of Action Research

The history of action research has been well documented and debated (c.f. Kemmis, 1990; Adelman, 1993; Noffke, 1994; and Gunz, 1996). Kurt Lewin (1890–1947) is frequently credited with coining the term "action research" in about 1934. After a series of practical experiences in the early 1940s, he came to view action research as a process that "gives credence to the development of powers of reflective thought, discussion, decision and action by ordinary people participating in collective research on 'private troubles' that they have in common" (Adelman, 1993, p. 8).

The many "descendants" of early action researchers follow different schools of action research thought, including the American action research group, with its roots in the progressive education movement—particularly in the work of John Dewey (Noffke, 1994); the efforts in the United Kingdom toward curriculum reform and greater professionalism of teaching (Elliott, 1991); and the Australian efforts located within a broad-ranging movement toward collaborative curriculum planning (Kemmis, 1990).

As is evident, the geographical locations and socio-political contexts in which action research efforts continue to evolve vary greatly. However, the primary focus of all of these efforts, regardless of the context, is on enhancing the lives of the children in our schools. As Noffke (1994) reminds us, reading the accounts of action research written by people housed in universities does little to illuminate the classroom experiences of teachers and what they hope to gain from participating in action research activities. Therefore, this book focuses on teachers examining issues related to the education of children and on partnering with teachers, administrators, counselors, and parents in the action research process.

Theoretical Foundations of Action Research

The theoretical perspectives and philosophies that inform the practices of teacher researchers today are as varied as the historical roots for action research. In the following section, we will briefly review the two main theories of action research: critical (or theory-based) action research and practical action research.

Critical Action Research

Critical action research is also known as emancipatory action research because of its goal of liberation through knowledge gathering. The term *critical action research* derives its name from the body of critical theory on which it is based, *not* because this type of action research is critical, as in "faultfinding" or "important," although it may certainly be both! The rationale for critical action research is provided by critical theory in the social sciences and humanities and by theories of postmodernism.

Critical theory in the social sciences and humanities and action research share several fundamental purposes (Kemmis, 1990). These similar interests or "commonalities of intent" include

1. A shared interest in processes for enlightenment.
2. A shared interest in liberating individuals from the dictates of tradition, habit, and bureaucracy.
3. A commitment to participatory democratic processes for reform.

In addition to its roots in the critical theory of the social sciences and humanities, critical action research also draws heavily from a body of theory called **postmodernism.** The postmodern perspective challenges the notions of truth and objectivity that the traditional scientific method relies so heavily upon. Instead of claiming the incontrovertibility of fact, postmodernists argue that truth is relative, conditional, and situational, and that knowledge is always an outgrowth of prior experience. For example, historically there has been little or no connection between research and practice in education—an apparent failure of research to affect teaching. This is not news for teachers! Research has been viewed as something done *on* them, not *for* them. The lack of influence of research on practice has been attributed to the following qualities of educational research

- It is not persuasive and has lacked the qualities of being compelling to teachers.
- It has not been relevant to teachers' daily practices—it has lacked practicality.
- It has not been expressed in ways that are accessible to teachers (Kennedy, 1997).

The postmodern perspective addresses many of these concerns by advocating for research that challenges the *taken-for-granted assumptions* of daily classroom life and presenting *truths* that are relative, conditional, situational, and based on prior experience. So while research might provide insights into promising practices (from research conducted in *other* teachers' classrooms and schools), action research conducted in your *own* classroom/school is more likely to be persuasive, relevant, and the findings expressed in ways that are meaningful for you and your colleagues.

Postmodern theory pulls apart and examines the mechanisms of knowledge production and questions many of the basic assumptions on which modern life is based. It thus inspires us "to examine the ordinary, everyday, taken-for-granted ways in which we organize and carry out our private, social, and professional activities" (Stringer, 1996, p. 156). Action research gives us a means by which we can undertake this examination and represent the experiences of classroom teachers that are contextually and politically constructed.

The values of critical action research dictate that all educational research should be socially responsive as well as

1. Democratic—Enabling participation of people.
2. Equitable—Acknowledging people's equality of worth.
3. Liberating—Providing freedom from oppressive, debilitating conditions.
4. Enhancing—Enabling the expression of people's full human potential. (Stringer, 1993, p. 148).

While this critical theory-based approach has been criticized by some for lack of practical feasibility (Hammersley, 1993), it is nonetheless important to consider because this important perspective provides a helpful heuristic, or problem-solving approach, for teachers who are committed to investigate through action research the taken-for-granted relationships and practices in their professional lives. Key Concepts Box 1-2 summarizes the most important components of a critical perspective of action research.

Components of a Critical Perspective of Action Research	
KEY CONCEPT	**EXAMPLE**
Action research is participatory and democratic.	You have identified an area in your teaching that you believe can be improved (based on data from your students). You decide to investigate the impact of your intervention and to monitor if it makes a difference.
Action research is socially responsive and takes place in context.	You are concerned that minority children (for example ESL [English as Second Language] students) in your classroom are not being presented with curriculum and teaching strategies that are culturally sensitive. You decide to learn more about how best to teach ESL children and to implement some of these strategies.
Action research helps teacher researchers examine the everyday, taken-for-granted ways in which they carry out professional practice.	You have adopted a new mathematics problem-solving curriculum and decide to monitor its impact on student performance on open-ended problem-solving questions and students' attitudes toward mathematics in general.
Knowledge gained through action research can liberate students, teachers, and administrators and enhance learning, teaching, and policy making.	Your school has a high incidence of student absenteeism in spite of a newly adopted district-wide policy on absenteeism. You investigate the perceptions of colleagues, children, and parents toward absenteeism to more fully understand why the existing policy is not having the desired outcome. Based on what you learn, you implement a new policy and systematically monitor its impact on absenteeism levels and students' attitudes toward school.

Practical Action Research

Practical action research places more emphasis on the "how-to" approach to the processes of action research and has a less "philosophical" bent. It assumes, to some degree, that individual teachers or teams of teachers are autonomous and can determine the nature of the investigation to be undertaken. It also assumes that teacher researchers are committed to continued professional development and school improvement and that teacher researchers want to systematically reflect on their practices. Finally, the practical action research perspective assumes that as decision makers, teacher researchers will choose their own areas of focus, determine their data collection techniques, analyze and interpret their data, and develop action plans based on their findings. These beliefs are summarized in Key Concepts Box 1-3.

Components of a Practical Perspective of Action Research	
KEY CONCEPT	**EXAMPLE**
Teacher researchers have decision-making authority.	Your school has adopted a school-based decision-making approach that provides teachers with the authority to make decisions that most directly impact teaching and learning. Given this decision-making authority, you decide as part of your continued professional development to investigate the effectiveness of a newly adopted science curriculum on students' process skills and attitudes.
Teacher researchers are committed to continued professional development and school improvement.	Based on the results of statewide assessment tests and classroom observations, the teachers and principal at your school determine that reading comprehension skills are weak. Collaboratively, the staff determines the focus for a school improvement effort and identifies the necessary professional development that will be offered to change the ways teachers teach reading.
Teacher researchers want to reflect on their practices.	You are a successful classroom teacher who regularly reflects on your daily teaching and what areas could be improved. You believe that part of being a professional teacher is the willingness to continually examine your teaching effectiveness.
Teacher researchers will use a systematic approach for reflecting on their practice.	Given a schoolwide reading comprehension focus, you have decided to monitor the effectiveness of a new reading curriculum and teaching strategies by videotaping a reading lesson (once a month), administering reading comprehension "probes" (once a week), interviewing children in your classroom (once a term), and administering statewide assessment tests (at the end of the school year).
Teacher researchers will choose an area of focus, determine data collection techniques, analyze and interpret data, and develop action plans.	To continue the example above, you have focused on the effectiveness of a new reading curriculum and teaching strategies. You have decided to collect data using videotapes of lessons, regular "probes," interviews, and statewide assessment tests. During the year you try to interpret the data you are collecting and decide what it suggests about the effectiveness of the new curriculum and teaching strategies. When all of the data has been collected and analyzed, you decide what action needs to be taken to refine, improve, or maintain the reading comprehension curriculum and teaching strategies.

Although the critical/postmodern and practical theories of action research draw on vastly different worldviews, these two distinctly different philosophies of action research are united by common goals. These common goals go a long way toward bridging whatever philosophical, historical, social, and regional variations exist.

Action research done according to both philosophies creates opportunities for all involved to improve the lives of children and learn about the craft of teaching. All action researchers, regardless of their particular school of thought or theoretical position, are committed to looking critically at what we do in our classrooms and the effects our actions have on the children in our care.

By now it should be evident to you that educational change that *enhances the lives of children* is a main goal of action research. But action research can also *enhance the lives of professionals*.

Osterman and Kottkamp (1993) provide a wonderful rationale for action research as a professional growth opportunity in their "credo for reflective practice":

1. Everyone needs professional growth opportunities.
2. All professionals want to improve.
3. All professionals *can* learn.
4. All professionals are capable of assuming responsibility for their own professional growth and development.
5. People need and want information about their own performance.
6. Collaboration enriches professional development. (p. 46)

Action research is largely about developing the *professional disposition* of teachers, that is, encouraging teachers to be continuous learners—in their classrooms and in their practice. While action research is not a universal panacea for the intractability of educational reform, it is an important component of the professional disposition of teachers because it provides teachers with the opportunity to model for their students how knowledge is created.

Action research is also about incorporating into your daily routine a *reflective stance*—the willingness to look critically at your teaching so that you can improve or enhance it. It is about a commitment to the principle that as teachers we are always distanced from the ideal but are striving toward it anyway—it's the very nature of education! Action research significantly contributes to the professional stance that teachers adopt because it encourages them to examine the dynamics of their classrooms, ponder the actions and interactions of students, validate and challenge existing practices, and take risks in the process. When teachers gain new understandings about both their own and their students' behaviors through action research, they are empowered to

- Make informed decisions about what to change and what not to change.
- Link prior knowledge to new information.
- Learn from experience (even failures).
- Ask questions and systematically find answers (Fueyo & Koorland, 1997).

This goal of teachers to be professional problem solvers who are committed to improving both their own practice and student outcomes provides a powerful reason to practice action research.

Justifying Action Research: The Impact of Action Research on Practice

At the beginning of a course on action research, I often ask teachers to reflect on what they do in their schools and classrooms, that is, what are the assumptions they take for granted in their schools and what are the origins of those practices. Often the responses include

It's important to do the "skill" subjects in the morning and the "social" subjects in the afternoon in elementary schools because that's when young children can concentrate and learn more.

The best way to do whole-group instruction with young children (K–3) is to have them sit on the "mat" in a circle. That way they are close to the teacher and pay more attention to what is being said.

In high schools the optimal time for a learning period is forty-three minutes. Anything longer than that and the students get restless and lose concentration. Therefore, I think that the proposal for "block scheduling" is just an attempt to make us more like elementary school teachers.

If you simply share scoring guides with children, they will automatically do better on the test. There's no need to change instructional approaches.

While these are real examples of just a few of the naive theories about teaching and learning that I have heard, they also indicate the gap that has existed between research and practice in the field of education. Just how much of our teaching practice has been informed by research? Is our craft informed by folklore? Do we acquire our culture of teaching through years of participation and observation, first as students and then as neophyte teachers? How did teachers get to be the way they are? Are the Hollywood portrayals of teachers and teaching (for example, as shown in *Ferris Bueller's Day Off, Mr. Holland's Opus*, etc.) really warranted? What is it about research that makes teachers, in general, snicker at the thought that it can in some way improve practice? What is the potential for this discussion to put action into our action research efforts?

Research into the connection between research and practice and the apparent failure of research to affect teaching has provided the following insights:

- Teachers do not find research persuasive or authoritative.
- Research has not been relevant to practice and has not addressed teachers' questions.
- Findings from research have not been expressed in ways that are comprehensible to teachers.

- The education system itself is unable to change, or conversely, it is inherently unstable and susceptible to fads (Kennedy, 1997).

Many teacher researchers may consider Kennedy's hypotheses to be statements of the obvious; however, they provide yet another rationale for why many of us have chosen to be reflective practitioners: to address the intractability of the educational system. These hypotheses also speak to our desire to put action into our ongoing action research efforts.

Action Research Is Persuasive and Authoritative

Research done by teachers for teachers involves collection of persuasive data. They are persuasive because teachers are invested in the legitimacy of the data collection, that is, they have identified data sources that provide persuasive insights into the impact of an intervention on student outcomes. Similarly, the findings of action research and the actions recommended by them are authoritative for teacher researchers. In doing action research, teacher researchers have developed solutions to their own problems. The teachers—not outside "experts"—are the authorities on what works in their classrooms.

Action Research Is Relevant

The relevance of research published in journals to the real world of teachers is perhaps the most common concern raised by teachers when asked about the practical applications of educational research. Either the problems investigated by researchers are not the problems teachers really have, or the schools or classrooms in which the research was conducted are not even close to their own school environment. In reviewing the last two decades of research on schools and teaching, however, Kennedy (1997) cites the seminal works of Jackson's (1968) *Life in Classrooms* and Lortie's (1975) *Schoolteacher* as ways to illustrate the relevance of the findings of these studies. These findings were that classroom life was characterized by crowds, power, praise, and uncertainty:

- Crowds—Students are always grouped with twenty or thirty others, which means that they must wait in line, wait to be called on, and wait for help.
- Power—Teachers control most actions and events and decide what the group will do.
- Praise—Teachers also give and withhold praise so that students know which students are favored by the teacher.
- Uncertainty—The presence of twenty to thirty children in a single classroom means there are twenty to thirty possibilities for an interruption in one's work (Kennedy, 1997).

Kennedy goes on to argue that one of the aims of research is to increase certainty by creating **predictability** within the classroom, "Routines increase predictability and decrease anxiety for both teachers and students" (1997, p. 6).

One of the outcomes of action research is that it satisfies the desire that all teachers have to increase the predictability of what happens in their classrooms—

in particular, to increase the likelihood that a given curriculum, instructional strategy, or use of technology will positively affect student outcomes. And while these desirable outcomes come at the initial expense of predictability, that is, they have emerged from the implementation of a *new* intervention or innovation, the findings of your action research inquiries will, over time, contribute to the predictability of your teaching environment.

With Action Research, Teachers Have Access to Research Findings

Kennedy also hypothesizes that the apparent lack of connection between research and practice is due to teachers' poor access to research findings. This apparent lack of impact of research on teaching is, in part, credited to teachers' prior beliefs and values and the realization that teachers' practices cannot simply be changed by informing them of the results of a study. After all, if we reflect on how we currently teach and what we hold as sacred teaching practices, we are likely to find that our beliefs and values stem from how we were taught as children ("It worked for me and I'm successful. I'm a teacher.") and how we have had teaching modeled for us through our teaching apprenticeships (student teaching).

Simply informing teachers about research is unlikely to bring about change. Therein lies the beauty, power, and potential of action research to positively affect practice. As a teacher researcher you challenge your taken-for-granted assumptions about teaching and learning. Your research findings are meaningful to you because *you* have identified the area of focus. *You* have been willing to challenge the conventional craft culture. In short, *your* willingness to reflect on and change your thinking about your teaching has led you to become a successful and productive member of the professional community.

Action Research Challenges the Intractability of Reform of the Educational System

The final hypothesis offered by Kennedy (1997) is that the lack of connection between research and practice can be attributed to the education system itself, not the research. The educational system has been characterized as follows:

- A system for which there is a lack of agreed-on goals and guiding principles.
- A system that has no central authority to settle disputes.
- A system that is continually bombarded with new fads and fancies.
- A system that provides limited evidence to support or refute any particular idea.
- A system that encourages reforms that are running at cross-purposes to each other.
- A system that gives teachers (in the USA) less time than most other countries to develop curricula and daily lessons (Kennedy, 1997).

Given this characterization it is little wonder that the more things change, the more they stay the same! Again, action research gives teacher researchers the opportunity to embrace a problem-solving philosophy and practice as an integral part of the culture of their schools and their professional disposition and to challenge the intractability of educational reform by making action research a part of the system, rather than one more fad.

Action Research Is Not a Fad

One insight that Kennedy does not address when discussing the apparent failure of research to affect teachers' practices is the belief of many classroom teachers that researchers tend to investigate trendy fads and are interested only in the curricular approach or instructional method "du jour." Therefore, you may not be surprised to hear critics of action research say: "Why bother? This is just another fad that, like other fads in education, will eventually pass if I can wait it out!" But action research is decidedly not a fad for one simple reason: *Good teachers have always systematically looked at the effects of their teaching on student learning.* They may not have called this practice action research, and they may not have thought their reflection was formal enough to be labeled *research,* but action research it was!

Making Action Research a Part of Your Daily Teaching Practice

The first step in making action research a part of your daily teaching practice is to familiarize yourself with the process and recognize how much action research you already do in your daily life as a classroom teacher. Consider this analogy that reveals how similar the act of teaching is to the act of doing action research. In any individual lesson, you plan, implement, and evaluate your teaching, just as a teacher researcher does when undertaking action research. You develop a list of objectives (a focus area), implement the lesson, reflect on whether the children achieved the objectives through summative evaluation statements (data collection), spend time at the end of a lesson reflecting on what happened (data analysis and interpretation), and spend time at the end of the day considering how today's lesson will affect tomorrow's lesson (action planning). Like action research, the act of teaching is largely an intuitive process carried out idiosyncratically by experienced and novice teachers alike.

I was recently reminded by a teacher enrolled in one of my action research classes that in my fervor and enthusiasm to illustrate data analysis and interpretation in practice (based on some of my own research) I had unwittingly made her feel that research was something that could realistically be done only by a full-time researcher who didn't have a "real" job to contend with—namely teaching twenty-eight very lively first graders! The teacher felt convinced that action research was so difficult and time-consuming that it was unreasonable to expect a mere mortal to undertake the activity. She felt as if she needed "Super Teacher" to burst into the classroom and take over business! Not so. If the process of action research cannot be done without adversely affecting the fundamental work of teaching, then it ought not to be done at all.

Throughout this text, we will explore practical, realistic ways that action research can become a normative part of the teaching-learning process. There will be an initial commitment of time and energy as we learn how to do action research, but that time is an investment in enhancing the lives of the children we teach. As a teacher, if you are going to realistically incorporate the process of action research into your daily teaching practices, a few things need to happen.

Try the Process and Be Convinced that the Investment of Time and Energy Are Worth the Outcomes. First, undertake an action research project that is meaningful to you and addresses the needs of your students. Once you have completed the project, you will see the contribution your new understanding of the subject will make to your teaching or your students' learning (or ideally, both!). Only then will you be fully confident that action research is a worthwhile investment of your time and energy. You will change your beliefs and attitudes about action research once you have tried it for yourself.

Know that Action Research Is a Process that Can Be Undertaken Without Having a Negative Impact on Your Personal and Professional Life. For example, action research as it is described in this book is not intended to be just "one more thing" for you to do. Teachers already have too much to do and not enough time in which to do it! The action research process advocated in this book is intended to provide you with a systematic framework you can apply to your daily teaching routines. The investment of time as you learn how to do action research will hopefully be worth the outcomes. The process may also produce unexpected positive outcomes by providing opportunities for collaborative efforts with colleagues who share a common "area of focus." This book will provide you with strategies you can use to develop your *reflective practice* utilizing many of the existing data sources in your classroom and school. It will also provide you with a model you can share with like-minded colleagues who are committed to improving the teaching-learning process in their classrooms as well.

Ask for Support From Your Professional Colleagues with Implementation. Although studying theory, observing demonstrations, and practicing with feedback enable most teachers to develop their skills to the point that they can use a model fluidly, skill development by itself does not ensure transfer. Relatively few persons who obtain skill in new approaches to teaching will make that skill a part of their regular practice unless they receive coaching (Joyce, Hersh, & McKibben, 1983). That is why it is critical to your success as an action researcher that you do action research and seek support and guidance from other teacher-researchers as you do it. These suggestions are summarized in Research in Action Checklist 1-1.

RESEARCH IN ACTION CHECKLIST 1-1

Making Action Research a Part of Your Daily Teaching Practice

_____ Actually *try* the process to convince yourself that the investments of time and energy are worth the outcomes.

_____ Recognize that action research is a process that can be undertaken without negatively affecting your personal and professional life.

_____ Seek support from your professional colleagues.

The Process of Action Research

Now that you know what action research is, what its historical and theoretical foundations are, and why teachers do it, let's explore the process of action research. Many guidelines and models have been provided over the years for teacher researchers to follow:

- Kurt Lewin (1952) described a "spiraling" cyclical process that included planning, execution, and reconnaissance.
- Stephen Kemmis (1990) has created a well-known representation of the action research "spiral" (see Figure 1-1) that includes the essential characteristics of

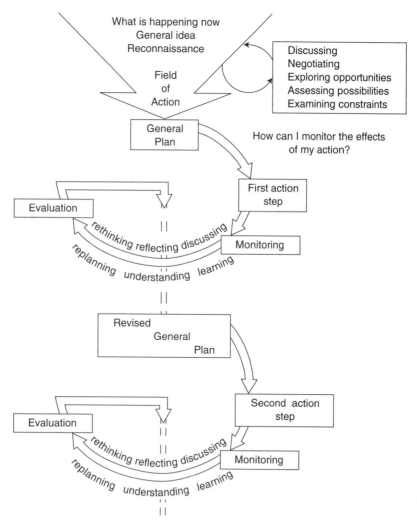

FIGURE 1-1   A Representation of Lewin's Action Research Cycle

From *Action Research in Retrospect and Prospect,* p. 29, by Stephen Kemmis, 1990. Victoria, Australia: Deakin University Press. Copyright ©1990 Deakin University Press. Reprinted with permission. All rights reserved.

Lewin's model. Kemmis' model includes reconnaissance, planning, first action step, monitoring, reflecting, rethinking, and evaluation.

- Richard Sagor (1992) has described a sequential, five-step process that includes problem formulation, data collection, data analysis, reporting of results, and action planning.
- Emily Calhoun (1994) has described an Action Research Cycle (see Figure 1-2) that includes selecting an area or problem of collective interest, collecting data, organizing data, analyzing and interpretating data, and taking action.
- Gordon Wells (1994) has described what he calls an Idealized Model of the Action Research Cycle (see Figure 1-3) that includes observing, interpreting, planning change, acting, and "the practitioner's personal theory" (p. 27) that informs and is informed by the action research cycle.
- Ernest Stringer (1996) has described an Action Research Interacting Spiral (see Figure 1-4) that includes looking, thinking, and acting as a "continually recycling set of activities" (p. 17).

All of these models have enjoyed varying degrees of popularity depending on the context in which they have been applied. For example, these action research models have been applied to agriculture, health care, factory work settings, and community development in isolated areas.

Clearly, these action research models share some common elements: a sense of purpose based on a "problem" or "area of focus," (identify an area of focus), observation or monitoring of practice (collect data), synthesis of information gathered (analyze and interpret data), and some form of "action" that invariably "spirals" the researcher back into the process again, and again, and again (develop an action plan).

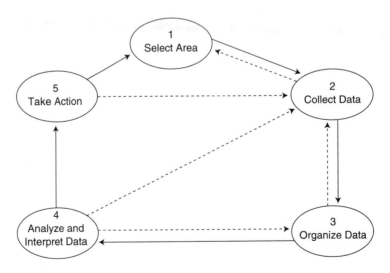

FIGURE 1-2 The Action Research Cycle

From *How to Use Action Research in the Self-Renewing School* by Emily Calhoun, 1994, Alexandria, VA: Association for Supervision and Curriculum Development. Copyright ©1994 ASCD. Reprinted by permission. All rights reserved.

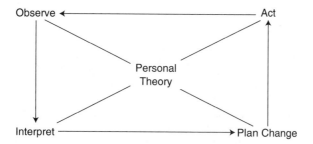

FIGURE 1-3   An Idealized Model of the Action Research Cycle

These shared elements are what we will focus on in this book. The following chapters will address in detail how to proceed with an action research process that includes the four elements mentioned above: **identifying an area of focus**, **data collection**, **data analysis and interpretation**, and **action planning**.

This four-step process, which I have termed the **Dialectic Action Research Spiral**, is illustrated in Figure 1-5. It provides teacher researchers with a practical guide and illustrates how to proceed with inquiries. It is a model for research done by teachers and for teachers and students, not research done *on* them, and as such is a dynamic and responsive model that can be adapted to different contexts and purposes. It was designed to provide teacher researchers with "provocative and constructive ways" of thinking about their work (Wolcott, 1989, p. 137).

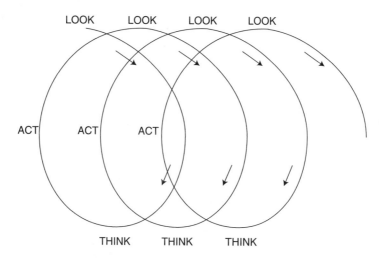

FIGURE 1-4   Action Research Interacting Spiral

Steps in the Action Research Process Based on Deborah South's Example of "Unmotivated" Students

KEY CONCEPT	EXAMPLE
Identifying an area of focus.	The purpose of this study was to describe the effects of a "study skills" curriculum on student outcomes. In particular, the study focused on the variables of student attendance, peer influence, adult influence, and students' self-esteem.
Collecting data.	Data was collected through surveys, interviews, and report card/attendance records.
Analyzing and interpreting the data.	Attendance did not appear to be an issue—children attended school regularly. Peer groups did affect performance. Students encouraged each other not to complete homework assignments. Teacher approval of student work appeared to have little effect on students' work habits, whereas about half of the children indicated that they were motivated to complete their homework to receive parental approval. On average, student grades had dropped dramatically during the term they were enrolled in the study skills class. Interpretation: The study skills class was having a negative impact on student outcomes, behavior, and attitudes.
Action planning.	It was determined that students would not be homogeneously grouped for a study skills class the following year because of a "critical mass of negativity" that appeared to emerge from the students as they fed off each other's lack of motivation. The study skills curriculum would continue to be used and monitored with a heterogeneous grouping of students.

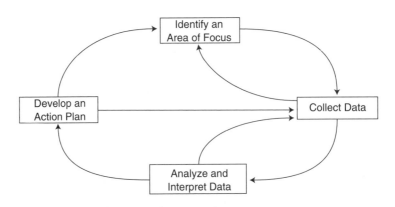

FIGURE 1-5 The Dialectic Action Research Spiral

Summary

Action research is systematic inquiry done by teachers (or other individuals in the teaching/learning environment) to gather information about—and subsequently improve—the ways their particular schools operate, how they teach, and how well their students learn.

The geographical settings and theoretical contexts in which action research efforts evolved are diverse. Two main philosophical perspectives inform current action research practice: **critical action research**, which has its roots in critical and postmodern theory and emphasizes democracy and liberation, and **practical action research**, which takes a more applied and contextualized approach to action research.

The shared goal for all types of action research is to improve the lives of both students and teachers. Classroom teachers are often skeptical of research because of its historical failure to connect to classroom practice and the experiences of teachers and students. Action research is not a passing fad because good teachers have always critically reflected upon their practices. This text will provide realistic strategies and practical guidelines for incorporating action research into teachers' daily classroom practices.

Although there are a number of models for doing action research, the basic process of doing action research consists of four steps: **identify an area of focus**, **collect data**, **analyze and interpret data**, and **develop an action plan**. The following chapters will explore these four steps in greater detail.

For Further Thought

1. How would you describe the purpose(s) of action research?
2. How do the tenets of the critical/postmodern perspective support the need for action research?
3. Suppose that the students in your class are not progressing in essay writing as you had hoped. Using the four steps in the action research process described in this chapter, sketch out briefly what you might do to systematically examine this issue.

CHAPTER 2

Deciding on an Area of Focus

This chapter provides guidelines for clarifying a general idea and area of focus for action research efforts. Procedures are described for doing reconnaissance and reviewing related literature using on-line resources such as ERIC, university library resources, or articles found in journals published by professional organizations for educators. Finally, this chapter tells how to create an action research plan.

———

After reading this chapter you should be able to

1. Select an appropriate area of focus.
2. Do reconnaissance.
3. Review related literature using on-line resources.
4. Write an action plan to guide your work.

Interactive Teen Theater
CATHY MITCHELL

Cathy Mitchell is a substitute teacher who also works with teen theater companies. Her story helps us to see how serendipity can play a role in developing an area of focus. In the beginning of the action research process, Cathy was not sure what her area of focus would be. However, as the result of an unexpected "intervention" to her teen theater production when an actor did not turn up for a performance, Cathy decided to systematically investigate the effects of improvisation on audience participation.

For the past ten years I have directed peer education teen theaters. These companies create and perform original plays based on company members' experiences and ideas. The plays are collections of dramatic scenes, comic sketches, and songs; the topics are current issues of concern to young people, including self-esteem, substance abuse, teen pregnancy, love versus lust, violence, family relationships, and sexually transmitted diseases. We tour extensively, performing for high schools and middle schools as well as at juvenile detention facilities.

While the company is generally very well received, I have felt that there is something stale in the actor/audience relationship. The audience sits attentively, laughs in recognition, and enjoys the variety in their class day, but remains essentially passive. Question sessions after the show, initially planned to generate discussion about important topics, frequently degenerated into boring adulation questions such as, "How long have you been rehearsing this?" or "Do you want to be an actor when you grow up?"

Two years ago, a few actors had to miss a performance. When we arrived at the high school we were scheduled to perform at, we realized the opening scene had two small roles that we could not eliminate but didn't have enough actors to fill. I asked two children from the audience to volunteer, taught them their lines backstage while the

rest of the scene was going on, and they walked on stage and finished the scene. The audience was instantly galvanized. Even with this very small change we had broken the division between actor and audience.

This began my experience into interactive theater. For me, this has meant bringing some of the improvisation techniques that we use to develop material during rehearsals onto the stage and inviting the audience to participate in limited ways. I found that involving the audience changed the dynamics from a passive spectator sport to a more participatory dialogue.

Through my research I have arrived at a working description for interactive theater: A short scene is played by workshop actors. The audience is asked to look for opportunities to improve the resolution. The scene is played again, and any time anyone wants to intervene and take any character's place to show a better way of handling the situation, they just shout "Stop!" and take over the role. One scene may be played many times. Often no closure is evident, and the scene ends in unresolved issues and heightened emotions. The actors and audience then discuss the issues generated by the scene.

The purpose of my study was to determine the effects of audience interaction with the actors in teen theater productions on their ability to identify issues and transfer learnings into similar problems in their lives. For example, in the current production of Duct Tape Theater, a company I direct, there is a well written scene called "Sticks and Stones," which is a collage containing poetry, a song, short monologues, and scenes. It lasts about 20 minutes and confronts issues of prejudice, discrimination, and violence. I decided as my intervention to replace this scene with an interactive theater piece developed with the audience. For three performances we included "Sticks and Stones" (my control groups), and for three other performances we included what became known as the "Violence Improv" audience interaction scene. This gave us six audiences: three control groups and three interactive groups.

Some of my methods of data collection for this project—my personal journal and the actors' journals, which are required for actors receiving credit for the class—were already in place. I also asked each teacher to write me a letter commenting on what they observed during the performance. But none of these gave me the data I really wanted but which was most difficult to collect—data from the audience. I decided to have my acting company develop this data collection source with me. The actors and I developed a questionnaire to be filled out directly after the performance and a group interview technique that involved three company members meeting with a small group of audience members for about 15 minutes. The goal was to generate as many responses as possible to the scenes about teen violence and harassment. One actor served as the interviewer, one as the scribe, and one kept a running tally of comments and responses.

The data showed three clear themes:

1. The audience clearly judged the performance containing the "Violence Improv" as more relevant to their lives than the control performance of "Sticks and Stones."
2. More individuals participated in discussing the issues of violence and harassment, with more overall comments and more comments that were considered "right on." This data showed that more audience members were able to both identify issues in the performance and to relate these issues to their own lives.

3. The clearest negative response was that the interactive piece made the performance feel "rushed." This data told me that the interactive material threw off the timing of the show. I often wrote in my own journal that I feel exhausted at the end of performances, and teachers wrote to me that we were running into break time and past the end of the period "trying to squeeze everything in."
4. The biggest letdown to me was that there wasn't any significant increase in the number of different issues identified or solutions suggested between the two audiences. Even though the interactive improvisation generated more answers and much more participation, the issues and solutions were pretty much the same.

My action research project confirmed to me that my methods for making teen theater work more meaningful are on the right track. It also became clear, however, that the format I am using is not the best one. I plan to continue working with the teen theater groups, to modify the format I have used in the past, and to monitor the effects of the changes on participants' transfer of learning to their real lives. For me, this is critical work. But for me, the most important result of this project is that I feel renewed energy for my work. Last year at this time I was busily seeking a replacement for myself and announcing to everyone that I wasn't going to direct teens anymore. I didn't even consider that I could examine the problem, address it, and remedy it. It feels really good to expect something to happen in my working life as a result of my own research and reflection.

∎

Not everyone comes to an action research setting with an area of focus in mind. In fact, many teachers initially resist participating in the process. It is not uncommon for teachers and administrators to skeptically claim, "I'm only here because I have to be. No action research—no teaching license!" In this teen theater example, the "intervention" and "area of focus" emerged quite unexpectedly and lead to some important understandings about how to increase audience understanding and participation.

We'll assume, then, that you may not have identified an area of focus. However, you probably do have several interests and concerns: perhaps your content area, a self-contained special education classroom, an at-risk program, an alternative education program, a multigraded classroom, a single fourth-grade classroom, a reading specialist program, a block-scheduled team teaching program, or even a one-room schoolhouse (to name a few)!

Every teacher and administrator who undertakes an action research project starts at the same place: making explicit a question or problem to investigate, or defining an **area of focus.** Finding an area of focus can be hard work if your action research inquiry is going to be engaging and meaningful for you. Taking time in the beginning to ensure that your topic is important—for you—is a critical step in the action research process. No one should tell you what your area of focus is or ought to be. The following guidelines can help you focus your research question.

Clarifying a General Idea and Area of Focus

In the beginning of the action research process, it is a good idea to clarify the "general idea" that will be the area of focus. The general idea is "a statement which links an idea to action" and "refers to a state of affairs or situation one wishes to change or improve on" (Elliott, 1991). Here are some examples, phrased in the form of a statement based on an observation, and followed by a question about how the situation could be improved:

- *Statement/Observation:* Students do not seem to be engaged during teen theater productions. *Question:* How can I improve their engagement?
- *Statement/Observation:* Students take a lot of time to learn problem solving in mathematics, but this process doesn't appear to transfer to their acquisition of other mathematics skills and knowledge. *Question:* How can I improve the integration and transfer of problem-solving skills in mathematics?
- *Statement/Observation:* Parents are unhappy with regular parent-teacher conferences. *Question:* How can I improve the conferencing process using student-led conferences?

Taking time in the beginning of the action research process to come to identify what you feel passionate about is critical. For some, this will be a relatively short activity—you may have come to an action research setting with a clear sense of a student-centered, teacher-centered, or parent-driven area of focus. For others, gaining a sense of the general idea will be more problematic. Don't rush it. Take time to talk to colleagues, reflect on your daily classroom life, and carefully consider what nags at you when you prepare for work every day.

Identifying Your Area of Focus
Is your area of focus an issue that
_____ Involves teaching and learning?
_____ Is within your locus of control?
_____ You feel passionate about?
_____ You would like to change or improve?

Criteria for Selecting a General Idea/Area of Focus

There are some important criteria you should keep in mind while identifying your general idea and subsequent area of focus (Elliott, 1991; Sagor, 1992):

- The area of focus should involve teaching and learning.
- The area of focus is something within your locus of control.
- The area of focus is something you feel passionate about.
- The area of focus is something you would like to change or improve.

Applying these criteria early in the process will keep you on track during the early stages of the action research process. They will also remind you of the vital and dynamic dimensions of action research—that it is important work done by teacher researchers for themselves and their students, the results of which will ultimately improve student outcomes. (See Research in Action Checklist 2-1.)

Reconnaissance

The next important step in the action research process is **reconnaissance,** or preliminary information gathering. More specifically, reconnaissance is taking time to reflect on your own beliefs and to understand the nature and context of your general idea. Doing reconnaissance takes three forms: self-reflection, description, and explanation.

Gaining Insight into Your Area of Focus Through Self-Reflection

First, try to explore your own understandings of

- The _theories_ that impact your practice.
- The _educational values_ you hold.
- How your work in schools fits into the _larger context_ of schooling and society.

- The *historical* contexts of your *school* and *schooling* and how things got to be the way they are.
- The *historical* contexts of how you came to *believe* what it is that you believe about *teaching* and *learning* (Kemmis & McTaggart, 1988).

If your general idea for your action research inquiry is the question: How can I improve the integration and transfer of problem-solving skills in mathematics? You might think about the following:

- Based on my experience teaching mathematics and my reading of the subject, I have been influenced by Van de Walle's (1994) *theory* about teaching and learning mathematics developmentally. In particular, the goal of mathematics is *relational understanding,* which is the connection between *conceptual* and *procedural knowledge* in mathematics. This theory of mathematics directly affects the ways I think about teaching mathematics to my children.
- I hold the *educational value* that children ought to be able to transfer problem-solving skills to other areas of mathematics as well to life outside of school. That is, I am committed to relevancy of curriculum.
- I believe that mathematical problem solving, and problem solving in general, fits the *larger context* of schooling and society by providing children with critical lifelong learning skills that can be transferred to all aspects of their life.
- The *historical context* of mathematics teaching suggests a rote method of memorizing facts and algorithms. While this approach to teaching mathematics worked for me (as a child and young teacher), it no longer suffices as a teaching method today.
- The historical context of how I came to believe in the importance of changing how I teach mathematics to children has grown out of my own frustration with knowing what to do to solve a problem, but not knowing *why* I need to use a particular approach or algorithm.

Given this self-reflection on an area of focus related to the integration and transfer of problem-solving skills in mathematics, I can now better understand the problem before I implement an intervention that addresses my concern for how to best teach a *relevant* problem-solving curriculum.

Gaining Insight into Your Area of Focus Through Descriptive Activities

Next, try to describe as fully as possible the situation you want to change or improve by focusing on *who, what, when,* and *where.* Grappling with these questions to clarify the focus area for your action research efforts will prevent moving ahead with an investigation that was too murky to begin with. For example, in this stage, you might answer these questions:

- What evidence do you have that this (the problem-solving skills of math students) is a problem?
- Which students are not able to transfer problem-solving skills to other mathematics tasks?

- How is problem solving presently taught?
- How often is problem solving taught?
- What is the ratio of time spent teaching problem solving to time spent teaching other mathematics skills?

Gaining Insight into Your Area of Focus Through Explanatory Activities

Once you've adequately described the situation you intend to investigate, try to explain it. Focus on the *why*. Can you account for the critical factors that have an impact on the general idea? In essence, this is the step in which you develop a hypothesis stating the expected relationships between variables in your study (Elliott, 1991).

In this case, you might hypothesize that students are struggling with the transfer of problem-solving skills to other mathematics tasks because they are not getting enough practice, they lack fundamental basic math skills, or that the use of math manipulatives has been missing or not used to its full potential. Given these possible explanations for why children have not been successfully transferring problem-solving skills to other areas of mathematics, you might develop the following hypotheses:

- There is a relationship between the use of a mathematics curriculum that emphasizes the children's ability to know *what* to do and *why* to do it and children's abilities to transfer problem-solving skills.
- There is a relationship between the use of a mathematics curriculum that emphasizes the use of manipulatives (to help children create meaning) and children's abilities to transfer problem-solving skills.

These reconnaissance activities (self-reflection, description, and explanation) help teacher researchers clarify what they already know about the proposed focus of the study; what they believe to be true about the relationships of the factors, variables, and contexts that make up their work environment; and what they believe can improve the situation. Research in Action Checklist 2-2 summarizes the critical activities for reconnaissance you should perform at this point in the action research process.

Review of Related Literature

At this point you should make an initial foray into the professional literature, the formal record of other people's experiences, to try to better understand the problem on which you are focusing. The literature may suggest other ways of looking at your problem and help you identify potential *promising practices* that you might use in your classroom to correct the problem. To borrow the words of Kemmis and McTaggart, "Can existing research throw any light on your situation, and help you see it more clearly?" (1988, p. 55).

There appears to be some debate among authors of action research books as to the importance of reviewing the literature as a strategy in the action research process. Most experts agree, however, that reviewing the literature is a valuable

RESEARCH IN ACTION CHECKLIST 2-2

Critical Activities for Doing Reconnaissance

Self-Reflection:

_____ Reflect on your area of focus in light of your values and beliefs; your understandings about the relationships between theory, practice, school, and society; how things got to be the way they are; and what you believe about teaching and learning.

Description:

_____ Describe the situation you wish to change or improve.

_____ Describe the evidence you have that the area of focus is a problem.

_____ Identify the critical factors that affect your area of focus.

Explanation:

_____ Explain the situation you intend to investigate by hypothesizing how and why the critical factors you've identified affect that situation.

---

activity for action researchers. For example, Sagor writes: "I would encourage anyone interested in doing good research to review the literature immediately after engaging in the problem-formulation activities" (1992). While reviewing the literature has long been a well-established component of dissertation and contract research and graduate research classes, its inclusion here signals the importance teacher researchers have awarded the activity.

Reviewing the literature is a valuable contribution to the action research process that could actually save you time. Often, teacher researchers think that they know what their problem is but become stymied in the process because they weren't really sure what they were asking. Taking time to immerse yourself in the literature gives you time to reflect on your own problems through someone else's lens. You can locate yourself within the research literature and find support for what you are doing or be challenged by what other researchers have done and how they have tackled a particular problem.

At the end of the process, you ought to be well informed about the literature to the degree that you could talk to colleagues about the major themes that emerged. Similarly, you should be able to talk about "promising practices" that were discussed.

You might also view this activity as being analogous to the exercise most people undertake before making a major purchase for their family—they immerse themselves in the literature to see what other folks have learned about a particular product. For example, I recently purchased a new automobile. My wife and I discussed the kind of vehicle we wanted in light of our family needs (one child), recreational interests (skiing in the winter and camping in the summer), and of course, budget (can we really afford a car payment?). In a sense, this activity was akin to selecting an area of focus. In our case, our area of focus was the purchase of a Sport Utility Vehicle (SUV). This lead me very naturally to review the related literature about SUVs in sources such as *Consumer Reports*, *Car and Driver*, *Edmund's Buying Guide* on-line, and the *Kelly Blue Book* for reviews and comparative pricing information.

This review of literature was an invaluable exercise for helping me see clearly the issues related to purchasing a SUV. For example: Did we really need all of the extras included on a particular vehicle? What size engine did we need to tow our tent trailer? How did the safety and reliability of different vehicles compare? As in action research, immersion in the related literature helps clarify all of the issues to consider when undertaking the solving of problems.

This activity also helped me identify "promising practices" for purchasing a new vehicle. For example, given the "sticker price," how much should I really pay for the vehicle? Again, the literature identified purchasing strategies that had been used by experienced buyers. These strategies included determining the manufacturer's cost of the vehicle to the dealer; accounting for dealer incentive programs, dealer "holdbacks," and manufacturer-to-buyer "cashback" incentives; and of course, how to calculate a "fair" price while still paying the dealer enough to cover advertising costs, commissions, and so on.

After reviewing this literature, I was prepared to implement a "promising practice" (buying strategy) for the SUV we had determined best met our needs and budget. And while the time spent immersing myself in the literature did not guarantee that my intervention would achieve my desired outcomes, I was better prepared to initiate my strategy and was informed about how I would know if I achieved my goals—based on what other experts in the field had done in the past.

Action researchers rely on three main sources of literature to better prepare themselves to undertake research: on-line searching of the Educational Resources Information Center (ERIC) and similar on-line resources, visits to a university library, and membership in professional organizations.

Educational Resources Information Center (ERIC)

Because many teachers work in isolated rural areas, and others simply do not have time to visit or convenient access to major research libraries, reviewing the literature can pose challenges. With increased personal and institutional access to the Internet, however, using the Educational Resources Information Center (ERIC) has become a popular strategy for teachers to use in locating current literature. With its user-friendly features, ERIC is a quick, easy way to get access to the related literature. (One of the drawbacks for discussing on-line searching is the rapidly changing nature of technology. However, while the following Internet addresses may change, the basic strategies for searching will not. With a basic level of computer literacy, any of us will be able to find sites on the Internet that serve our needs.)

Established in 1966 by the National Library of Education as part of the United States Department of Education's Office of Educational Research and Improvement, ERIC is the world's largest database on education. It provides information on subjects ranging from early childhood and elementary education to education for gifted children and rural and urban education. ERIC is used by more than 500,000 people each year, and with increasing access to the system through AskERIC on-line, this number is expected to grow dramatically.

Currently, ERIC is available a number of ways:

- By calling 1-800-LET-ERIC (1-800-538-3742).
- Via the Internet through the AskERIC Virtual Library.
- Through the AskERIC on-line question-and-answer service (askeric@ericir. syr.edu).
- Through the more conventional use of ERIC on CD-ROM (Compact Disk— Read Only Memory) that is available at most university libraries.

However, the best starting point for your ERIC explorations is probably the ERIC systemwide web page at: http://www.aspensys.com/eric, shown in Figure 2-1. This page includes hot links to all other ERIC-sponsored sites.

According to material published on the ERIC homepage, in recent years ERIC has

- Experienced phenomenal growth in the numbers of individuals served.
- Won several awards for its innovative use of Internet technology to support educators and parents.
- Established strong partnerships with the public and private sectors to expand services at no additional cost to taxpayers.
- Acquired, produced, and distributed thousands of documents and journal articles addressing areas of highest priority within the education community.

FIGURE 2-1   Screen Capture of ERIC Web Page (http://www.accesseric.org:81)

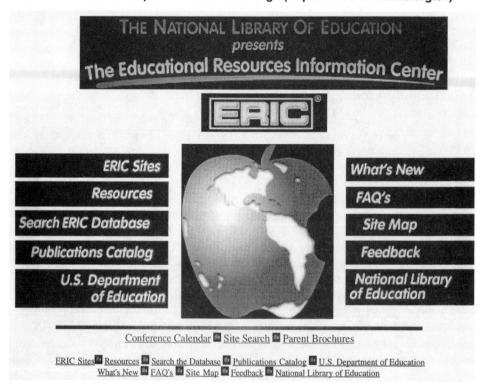

What makes ERIC all the more attractive to teacher researchers and university faculty is the fact that the on-line service to ERIC is currently free—there is no charge associated with conducting an ERIC search on-line from your home or school computer or for receiving on-line assistance with searching. Fees are incurred only if you place an order with ERIC. However, once you have identified the relevant literature, you may choose to simply access it at your university library and to make your own copies of journal articles or microfiche.

While a "full-text" ERIC system is in development (there are limited numbers of articles available in full text on-line), it may be some time before we are able to access the full text of all ERIC documents on-line. Presently, we have to settle for abstracts and selected articles that allow us to determine whether a particular article is relevant to our own investigations.

What Are the Limitations of Searching ERIC On-Line?

The strategies for searching ERIC on-line or by using a CD-ROM in your university library are very similar. The Education Librarian at my university believes that the "Silver Platter" CD-ROM is slightly more user friendly than ERIC on-line, but when questioned about the ways in which it was more user friendly he recounted with, "Perhaps it's more user friendly because there is a reference librarian present who can help with the search!" So, if the following discussion seems confusing, go to your nearest university library and request the assistance of a librarian to help you with your search; otherwise, venture into cyberspace and face the exciting opportunities associated with this virtual library.

There are indeed some limitations to searching ERIC on-line. For example, you are able to retrieve only a maximum of 100 citations at one time; most journal articles are available only through your local university library—not on-line; and the AskERIC database covers only the years 1989 to present, although earlier years are available on the CD-ROM indexes.

Finally, for those of you who are neophytes to the Internet—be warned—the Internet is a black hole that can suck up your time unless you remain focused on the task at hand. Overall, though, the ERIC on-line service is a good starting point in spite of the limitations, and the links to other sites you will encounter can help overcome some of the problems.

Conducting a Search Using ERIC On-Line

You can conduct a search using ERIC on-line in several ways: by using the AskERIC Service for Educators, the Search ERIC Wizard, the Expert Search Strategies, and by performing subject and keyword searches. Because the AskERIC Q&A Service for Educators is the easiest way for novices to gather information, we'll start there.

The AskERIC Service for Educators. AskERIC (http://ericir.syr.edu/Qa/) is a "personalized Internet-based service providing information to teachers, librarians, counselors, administrators, parents and others throughout the United States and the world" (ERIC Networker, 1998). The AskERIC Q&A service (askeric@askeric.org) responds to emails from individuals seeking information on educational theory and practice. Requests receive prompt (two-day) service from an ERIC information specialist who will respond with database citations, Internet resources, and if possible, full-text ERIC articles. For example, I emailed the AskERIC Q&A Service with the following request:

> I would like guidance on how best to search ERIC for literature on the effects of teaching elementary school children mathematical problem-solving skills on student achievement in other areas of mathematics, e.g., number and numeration, probability and statistics, geometry and visualization skills, and so on.

I quickly received the following response from AskERIC:

> Greetings,
> Thank you for sending your question to AskERIC! AskERIC is a unique service where questions are sent to a central address and then distributed to information specialists around the country. I am forwarding your question on to another ERIC facility that will respond to you shortly.

Within forty-eight hours of this response, I received the following detailed reply from Andrea Balas, an AskERIC specialist at the ERIC Clearinghouse at The Ohio State University:

> Greetings Geoff,
> In response to your request, I conducted a sample search of the ERIC database. Below I have appended my search strategy, citations with abstracts, and directions for accessing the full-text. These citations may represent an introductory, rather than exhaustive, search for information on your topic. You may wish to use those terms as you conduct your personal search on the ERIC web site. Using terms particular to your needs will help you find the information that meets your study; combinations of terms as in the sample search will help you do this. You may also wish to visit additional resource sites listed.
>
> If you would like to conduct your own free ERIC database searches via the Internet, please send a request for directions to askeric@ericir.syr.edu or go directly to http://ericir.syr.edu.
>
> Thank you for using AskERIC! If you have any questions or would like further assistance, please do not hesitate to send another message.

Included in this message was a description of how the search was conducted using keywords such as *mathematics*, *achievement*, *problem solving*, *probability*, *statistics*, and so on. This was followed by a list of ten associated web sites (like the National Council of Teachers of Mathematics), eleven citations and the abstracts for the articles (eight pages in length) that was a valuable starting point for my quest to learn more about the relationships between mathematical problem-solving skills and student achievement. This service provided a great starting point from which to immerse myself in the literature without leaving the relative comfort of my home, office, or school. Indeed, this is a far cry from the days of flipping through card catalogues and visiting the "stacks."

Search ERIC Wizard. Using this Wizard located at ericae2.educ.cua.edu/scripts/ewiz/amain2.asp, you can search the ERIC database at the ERIC Clearinghouse on Assessment and Evaluation and the ERIC Document Reproduction Service (EDRS). Click on the "Read this once" information for a full discussion of Wizard searching. In the searching process, it is critical that you use the correct ERIC descriptors in conducting your search. That is, you need to refer to the ERIC term for your area of focus, which may or may not match your meaning for the term. If you don't play by the ERIC rules, you will not be able to locate any articles that match what you are searching for, and you will have wasted a lot of time in the process.

For example, when I entered *problem solving* in the "Look up a new term" box, ERIC provided the following choices of other terms that could be used to correctly search ERIC: *cognitive processes, brainstorming, critical thinking, decision making, learning strategies, mathematical applications,* and *thinking skills* (ERIC provided forty choices in all!). Similarly, when I entered the term *student achievement,* ERIC responded that it didn't use *student achievement* as a descriptor and recommended that I search using *academic achievement.* This is a good example of where using a common term such as *student achievement* would not yield a useful search using the ERIC system. It is also a good example of the user-friendly nature of the ERIC Wizard that prompts the searcher to use the correct ERIC descriptor and other choices of descriptors from the ERIC Thesaurus.

The ERIC Wizard also offers Expert Search Strategies, sample search strategies on hot topics developed by some of the country's best reference librarians. These strategies incorporate the librarian's experience and in-depth knowledge of the ERIC database. By clicking on the link, you can load a strategy into the Search ERIC Wizard. You can then submit the search or modify it to meet your needs. (For more detailed instructions about customizing your search strategy, read the ERIC Help file.)

Subject Searches and Keyword Searches. Another quick way to search ERIC is by using a subject search. This is a specific search that uses the term you provide to search the ERIC database. If you are confident that you know the correct term (used by ERIC), then it is a simple case of entering the topic in the search box. However, if you are uncertain of the exact phrase used by ERIC for indexing a particular area, you can enter a keyword (your word) for searching the database. Using this technique may be more time consuming, but with persistence you will still conduct a good search.

Locating Materials You Have Identified Using ERIC On-Line

Once you have identified materials that you would like to examine using an ERIC on-line search, you need to get access to these materials.

You may notice in your searches that the results are categorized according to an ED or EJ designation. An ED designation is used for documents that are generally unpublished reports, studies, and even lesson plans. ED references are available in university libraries through ERIC's microfiche collection and can be ordered from the ERIC Document Reproduction Service (EDRS) in either electronic, microfiche, or paper format (http://edrs.com).

An EJ designation is used for articles that have been published in professional journals and can be located through reference to a periodicals catalogue or interlibrary loan. EJ articles are not available in full text from ERIC and must be copied by visiting a library, tracking down a copy of the particular journal, or using a document delivery service of which ERIC recommends a choice of three. The use of a document delivery service will be expensive compared to tracking down the journal article yourself.

While it is possible to order materials located through ERIC on-line, my advice (and the advice of ERIC) is to locate the materials at your local university library. This will save you a considerable amount of money; however, if the cost and time of traveling to a library are substantial, you may consider ordering documents on-line.

Other On-Line Resources

While ERIC is the largest database for searches of education literature, it is not the only source available. You should also consider a number of other sources, including Dissertation Abstracts International, PSYCHLIT, INFOTRAC, SEARCHBANK, and EBSCOHOST. Some of these sources, such as EBSCOHOST, are now offering articles in full text.

In addition, you can access other electronic indexing and abstracting sources by searching the Internet using your computer's search engine (for example, Lycos, Infoseek, Yahoo, and Excite). But be warned—there is little in the way of quality control for much that is found on the Internet (unless it is a refereed journal article). Be prepared to sift through piles of cyberspace junk to find the diamond in the rough.

Visiting a University Library

And of course, with all of this talk about user-friendly resources, don't overlook the most valuable, user-friendly resource of all—your university librarian! Most university libraries (and public libraries, for that matter) have a librarian on duty to help with requests. My university has an "education" librarian who has experience in both K–12 and graduate education and is very skilled in helping folks who are intimidated at the thought of navigating around the "stacks." However, if a librarian is not available when you make your initial visit, you are likely to find the following important resources that will allow you to start your work:

- **Computers.** Instead of the card catalogues that many of us remember using in the "old days" (funny how those old days become an increasingly frequent frame of reference!), you will now find a computer terminal that provides you with access to the library's resources. You may even be able to access other libraries with whom your institution has reciprocal loan agreements if a particular reference is not available at your home library. These electronic databases are extremely user friendly and give you a good place to start your search for literature related to your area of focus.
- **ERIC on CD-ROM.** The same computers that contain the library's electronic database may also provide access to a CD-ROM version of ERIC. You will be able to use the same search strategies outlined in the earlier "on-line" discussion.
- **Browsing the Stacks.** In all of this discussion about electronic databases, we have not considered the old strategy of browsing the stacks. This is similar to

the kind of activity you might undertake at a public library when looking for a new fiction book to read. If you can locate the area of the library with books related to your area of focus, it can be productive to browse and pull interesting books off the shelves. You may also find leads to related materials, not necessarily uncovered in your electronic search, by looking at any given book's reference list.

Membership in Professional Organizations

Perhaps the best way to access current literature related to your area of focus is through membership in professional organizations. The following list gives the names of a few professional organizations (U.S. based) that could be valuable resources for research reports and curriculum materials (in countries other than the United States there are likely to be national equivalents that could also be accessed through an Internet search). This list of professional organizations is not intended to be comprehensive for there are as many professional organizations as there are content areas (reading, writing, mathematics, science, social studies, music, health, and physical education, to name a few) and special interest groups (Montessori education, for example). A search of the Internet will provide a listing of more web sites than you will have the time or energy to visit!

- **Association for Supervision and Curriculum Development (ASCD) (http://odie.ascd.org).** Boasting 200,000 members in 100 counties, ASCD is one of the largest educational organizations in the world. According to their web site, ASCD is an international, nonprofit educational organization "committed to the mission of forging covenants in teaching and learning for the success of all learners." ASCD publishes books, newsletters, audiotapes, videotapes, and some excellent journals that are a valuable resource for teacher researchers, including *Educational Leadership* and *The Journal of Curriculum and Supervision*.
- **National Council of Teachers of Mathematics (NCTM) (http://nctm.org).** With 110,000 members, NCTM is dedicated to the teaching and learning of mathematics and offers vision and leadership for mathematics educators at all age levels. NCTM provides regional and national professional development opportunities and publishes the following journals: *Teaching Children Mathematics*, *Mathematics Teaching in the Middle School*, *Mathematics Teacher*, and the *Journal for Research in Mathematics Education*.
- **National Council for the Social Studies (NCSS) (http://www.ncss.org).** The NCSS also provides support for social studies teachers through the publication of the following journals: the *Journal of Social Education*, and *Social Studies and the Young Learner*.
- **National Science Teachers Association (NSTA) (http://nsta.org).** The NSTA, with 53,000 members, also provides many valuable resources for science teachers, including the National Science Education Standards and the following journals: *The Science Teacher*, *Science and Children*, and *Science Scope*.
- **International Reading Association (IRA) (http://www.ira.org).** The IRA provides resources to an international audience of reading teachers through its publication of the following journals: *The Reading Teacher*, *Journal of Adolescent and Adult Literacy*, and the *Reading Research Quarterly*.

Ideally, your investment of time and energy in the reconnaissance and review-of-the-literature stages will be rewarded with a synthesis of the related literature that helps you see your project more clearly. In addition, it may have helped you to identify "promising practices" that become an integral part of your ongoing action research efforts.

At this stage of the action research process, it is a good idea to create an action plan. An action plan summarizes your action research thoughts in a plan that will guide you through your action research work and includes the following nine steps:

1. Write an area-of-focus statement.
2. Define the variables.
3. Develop research questions.
4. Describe the intervention or innovations.
5. Describe the membership of the action research group.
6. Describe negotiations that need to be undertaken.
7. Develop a timeline.
8. Develop a statement of resources.
9. Develop data collection ideas. (adapted from Kemmis & McTaggart, 1988b, and Elliott, 1991)

Write an Area-of-Focus Statement

An area of focus identifies the purpose of your study. To start, write a statement that completes the following sentence: "The purpose of this study is to. . . ." For example:

- The purpose of this study is to describe the effects of an integrated problem-solving mathematics curriculum on student transfer of problem-solving skills and the retention of basic math facts and functions.
- The purpose of this study is to describe the impact of bringing audience members into an interactive relationship with teen theater productions on participants' abilities to identify issues and incorporate solutions to similar problems in their own lives.
- The purpose of this study is to describe the effects of student-led conferences on parent and student satisfaction with the conferencing process.

Define the Variables

As part of the area-of-focus statement construction process, write definitions of what you will focus on in the study. These definitions should accurately represent what the factors, contexts, and variables *mean to you*. A **variable** is a characteristic of your study that is subject to change. That is, it might be the way you are going to change how you teach, the curriculum you use, and student outcomes. Definitions may also emerge from the literature, but it is important that you own whatever you are defining and communicate that with others. In the preceding examples, the researchers would define what they mean by transfer of solutions to life's situations, an integrated problem-solving curriculum, transfer of problem-solving skills, the retention of math facts and functions, interactive participation in teen theater, student-led conferences, and parent and student satisfaction with the conferencing processes. If you are clear about what you are examining, it will be easy to determine how you will know it when you see it! That is, your data collection ideas will flow more freely and there will be no confusion when you communicate with your action research collaborators about your purpose.

Develop Research Questions

Develop questions that breathe life into the area-of-focus statement and help provide a focus for your data collection plan. These questions will also help you validate that you have a workable way to proceed with your investigation. For example:

- What is the effect of teen theater audience participation strategies on audience comprehension of issues?
- How does the "Violence Improv" affect audience understanding of the issues of violence and harassment?
- What is the effect of incorporating math manipulatives into problem-solving activities on student performance on open-ended problem-solving tests?
- In what ways do students transfer problem-solving skills to other areas of mathematics?
- How do students incorporate problem-solving skills into other curriculum areas?
- How do students transfer problem-solving skills to their life outside of school?

Describe the Intervention or Innovation

Describe what you are going to do to improve the situation you have described. For example, "I will implement a standards-based integrated problem-solving mathematics curriculum," "I will include audience improvisation as part of the teen theater performances I direct," and "I will incorporate student participation in student-parent-teacher conferences." Remember, this is simply a statement about what you will do in your classroom or school to address the teaching/learning issue you have identified.

Describe the Membership of the Action Research Group

Describe the membership of your action research group and discuss why its members are important. Will you be working with a site council team? A parent group? If so, what will be the roles and responsibilities of the group's participants? For example:

I will be working with seven other high school math teachers who are all members of the math department. While we all have different teaching responsibilities within the department, as a group we have decided on problem solving as an area of focus for the department. Each of us will be responsible for implementing curriculum and teaching strategies that reflect the new emphasis on problem solving and for collecting the kinds of data that we decide will help us monitor the effects of our teaching. The department chair will be responsible for keeping the principal informed about our work and securing any necessary resources we need to complete the research. The chair will also write a description of our work to be included in the school newsletter (sent home to all parents), thus informing children and parents of our focus for the year.

Describe Negotiations that Need to Be Undertaken

Describe any negotiations that you will have to undertake with others prior to implementing your plan. Do you need permission from an administrator? parents? students? colleagues? All of this assumes that you control the focus of the study and that you undertake the process of negotiation to head off any potential obstacles to implementation of the action plan. It's very frustrating to get immersed in the action research process only to have the project quashed by uncooperative colleagues or administrators.

Develop a Timeline

In developing a timeline, you will need to decide who will be doing *what*, *when*. Although not part of a timeline in the strictest sense, you can also use this stage to anticipate *where* and *how* your inquiry will take place. For example:

- **Phase 1 (August–October).** Identify area of focus, review related literature, develop research questions, reconnaissance.
- **Phase 2 (November–December).** Collect initial data. Analyze videotapes of lessons, do first interviews with children, administer first problem-solving probe.
- **Phase 3 (January–May).** Modify curriculum and instruction as necessary. Continue ongoing data collection. Schedule two team meetings to discuss early analysis of data.
- **Phase 4 (May–June).** Review statewide assessment test data and complete analysis of all data. Develop presentation for faculty. Schedule team meeting to discuss and plan action based on the findings of the study. Assign tasks to be completed prior to year two of the study.

Develop a Statement of Resources

Briefly describe what resources you will need to enact your plan. This is akin to listing materials in a lesson plan—there is nothing worse than starting to teach and finding you don't have all the manipulatives you need to achieve your objectives. For example, to participate in the study of math problem-solving skills, the team determines that it will need teacher release time for project planning, reviewing related literature, and other tasks; funds to purchase classroom sets of manipulatives; and a small budget for copying and printing curriculum materials. After all, there is no sense developing a study that investigates the impact of a new math problem-solving curriculum if you don't have the financial resources to purchase the curriculum.

Develop Data Collection Ideas

Give a preliminary statement of the kinds of data that you think will provide evidence for your reflections on the general idea you are investigating. For example, brainstorm the kind of intuitive, naturally occurring data that you find in your classroom or school, such as test scores, attendance records, portfolios, and anecdotal records. As we learn more about other types of data that can be collected, this list will grow, but in the early stages think about what you already have easy access to and then be prepared to supplement it with interviews, surveys, questionnaires, videotapes, audiotapes, maps, photos, and observations as the area of focus dictates.

These activities can be undertaken whether you are working individually, in a small group, or as part of a schoolwide action research effort. The resolution of these issues early in the action research process will ensure that you do not waste valuable time backtracking (or even apologizing) once you are well down the action research path. The process of developing an action plan is summarized in the Research in Action Checklist 2-3.

RESEARCH IN ACTION CHECKLIST 2-3

Developing an Action Plan
_____ Write an area-of-focus statement.
_____ Define the variables.
_____ Develop research questions.
_____ Describe the intervention or innovation.
_____ Describe the membership of the action research group.
_____ Describe negotiations that need to be undertaken.
_____ Develop a timeline.
_____ Develop a statement of resources.
_____ Develop data collection ideas.

Put the Action Plan into Action

Kemmis and McTaggart (1988b) provide the following conclusion to the process of developing a plan:

> Your plan orients you for action, of course; but it is also a reference point for reflection later on, and it is something which you can modify and develop in later plans. Since you have done so much hard thinking to put your plan together, don't skimp when it comes to drafting and redrafting it before you go into action. It represents the fruits of one round of reconnaissance and thinking ahead—it provides you with a benchmark for later reflection and replanning. (p. 77)

With the plan complete, it's time to determine what information (data) you can collect that will increase your understanding about your own practice and its impact on the children in your care. You are now ready to decide how you will monitor the effects of the innovation or intervention you are going to implement and to develop your data collection techniques.

Summary

Defining an area of focus, or making explicit the question or problem to investigate, is a critical step in the action research process. The process of articulating a meaningful area of focus involves doing reconnaissance (self-reflection, description, and explanation) and reviewing the related literature. You can use on-line resources such as ERIC (emailing the AskERIC Q&A Service for Educators at askeric@askeric.org is the easiest way to get started), visit a university library, or review the publications issued by professional organizations for educators to gain context for your action research inquiry.

After defining your area of focus, doing reconnaissance, and reviewing the literature, the next step is to write an action plan to guide your action research efforts. The action plan should include the following nine steps: Write an area-of-focus statement; define the variables; develop research questions; describe the intervention or innovation; describe the membership of the action research group; describe negotiations that need to be undertaken; develop a timeline; develop a statement of resources; and develop data collection ideas (adapted from Kemmis & McTaggart, 1988b, and Elliott, 1991).

For Further Thought

1. What general ideas do you have for action research?
2. What is your area of focus?
3. Complete the following statement: "The purpose of the study is to. . . ."
4. Complete an action plan that includes an area-of-focus statement, definitions, research questions, a description of the intervention, membership of the action research group, negotiations to be undertaken, a timeline, the necessary resources for the project, and data collection ideas.

CHAPTER 3

Data Collection Techniques

This chapter introduces qualitative data collection techniques that can be used to systematically investigate an area of focus. These techniques include using direct observation, interviews, questionnaires, attitude scales, and new and existing records and artifacts.

———

After reading this chapter you should be able to

1. Identify multiple data collection techniques to be included for each research question.
2. Develop the research instruments needed to begin your research.

Reflection on Action Research
JAMES ROCKFORD

James Rockford is an elementary teacher in a rural school district in Oregon. James is primarily responsible for teaching music and computer keyboarding skills to young children and initially became involved with action research as part of a statewide action research initiative. As a result of his first attempt at doing action research and his effort to make it a standard part of his teaching, James has also worked as a mentor for other teachers in his region. James' story highlights the importance of collecting data from a variety of sources to fully understand the effects of an intervention on student outcomes.

It seemed to be a perfect match. I had charge of a new computer lab and a mandate to develop a program of instruction to match the curriculum guide, and I needed a "problem" for a collaborative action research class that began in the Spring of 1995.

The only software that came with the computers was a popular program to teach keyboarding and Clarisworks. It didn't make any sense to spend several thousand dollars to teach keyboarding, so the problem became "How does keyboarding instruction enhance students' ability to use word processing, database, spreadsheet, and draw functions?"

Looking at the literature proved to be a formidable problem because there wasn't a good academic library in the area. The local community college had one on-line computer to access ERIC (Educational Resources Information Center) through the World Wide Web if I gave search terms to the librarian. A little help came, but I preferred to do the search myself. Our school was not yet on-line, so I resorted to using my son's computer. A quick survey of the literature showed plenty of research on keyboarding, but not much focused on young children. Opinions ranged from "start them as early as possible" to "avoid bad habits" to "don't bother

because they can hunt and peck as fast as they can type".

The problem proved to be a little overwhelming in that I had just started an instructional program to teach all the keyboarding skills, and it became obvious that results would be harder to get for database, spreadsheet, and draw functions. As a result, I decided to look initially only at the effect of teaching keyboarding on word processing for students in grades 4 through 6.

This was supposed to be a collaborative venture, so my first task was to enlist the help of the teachers in grades 4 through 6. We met after school one afternoon so I could explain the purpose of the project. They agreed to help gather data, but only one class actually got into the lab every day. This was disappointing, but it helped make the project more manageable since I would be handling data only from one class instead of three.

What variables might have an effect on students' success in learning to keyboard? I conducted a survey of teacher attitudes and a survey to assess whether students had any prior knowledge, how much time they spent on a computer at home and at school, and whether they had a computer at home. Records were kept for time on computers at school in instructional and free-choice situations.

A well-designed action research project should, as its name declares, lead to some kind of action. The purpose of my action research project was to determine if teaching keyboarding skills to sixth-grade students had enough of an impact on their word processing skills to warrant spending the time and money. It seemed rather obvious that it would, but several students had developed their own unique "hunt-and-peck" system and could already approach the district-mandated target of twenty words per minute. There are many variables that might affect word processing rates and that led to the following questions:

1. Do students have a computer at home? How much time do they spend at it per week?
2. What preexisting knowledge do students have about computers?
3. How much time do students spend at the computer when they're at school? How does it affect word processing rates?
4. What is the effect of the keyboarding software used in the lab at school?

The questions were then placed in a data matrix and triangulated as follows (Note: D.S. = data source):

Questions	D.S. 1	D.S. 2	D.S. 3
Preexisting knowledge?	Students' survey	Computer knowledge pretest	
Keyboarding speed?	Pretest	Posttest	Teacher help
Appropriate use (WP)?	Pretest software	Posttest software	Timed typing teacher constructed
Time on computers?	School lab records	Student survey	Parent survey

I collected data using surveys that I developed to measure the following areas:

- Student self-evaluation questionnaire.
- Teacher-constructed vocabulary/facts pretest of general computer knowledge.
- Teacher-constructed timed typing test rates.
- A classroom teacher survey of knowledge/ attitudes about technology.
- A teacher observation record for the computer lab.
- Existing records of students' word processing rates with software.
- Parent survey of student computer use outside of school.

Data were compiled as follows:

- The three variables of time, prior knowledge, and use of keyboarding software were analyzed using a scatter plot graph to determine any correlation to word processing speed.
- Surveys were compiled to show tendencies.
- Keyboarding rates between October and May were compiled in graph form to show progress over time.

In general the data indicated the following:

- Student time on computers out of school had no effect on word processing rate. (They love those computer games!)
- Time on computers at school was critical.
- In only one month, the class word processing rate mean had increased 300%.

As a result, it was apparent that the keyboarding software was effective, and on that basis I continued its use. Because time on task is critical, teachers were urged to take students to the lab every day and monitor keyboarding habits as well as install keyboarding software on classroom computers so that each student received a minimum of ten minutes practice per day. Timed typing tests require greater and different skills than are called for on keyboarding software. In the future, timed typing tests will be given weekly to provide an authentic assessment of student progress, and a tracking system will be used to monitor the acquisition of skill development.

Any research worth its salt appears to generate more questions than it answers. At the completion of this project, I was left wondering if a student's learning style had any impact on the ability to learn word processing skills. Would keyboarding instruction improve students' use of database, spreadsheet, and draw/paint functions? Could other types of authentic assessment be used to determine skill/concept development? These are questions I will continue to investigate.

The project became a springboard to address issues in setting up a computer lab. Instead of being behind the eight ball, I was able to anticipate

Student Self-Evaluation Survey

1. Do you have a computer that you use outside of school?

   (a) Yes   (b) No

2. How many hours a day do you spend at the computer outside of school?

   (a) 0   (b) 1 or less   (c) 1–2   (d) 2–3

3. How much time do you spend at the computer while you're at school?

   (a) 0   (b) 15 minutes   (c) 30 minutes   (d) more than 30 minutes

4. When you type on a keyboard, do you look at the

   (a) monitor (b) keyboard   (c) rough draft   (d) your neighbor

5. I use the computer to (circle all that apply)

   (a) play games   (b) write stories and reports
   (c) draw pictures   (d) collect information and store it
   (e) find information in the library

6. Learning to keyboard in the lab made my life with computers

   (a) easier   (b) more frustrating   (c) no different

7. If I had the chance to do more with computers, I would

   _____

8. The best thing about learning to keyboard is

   _____

9. The hardest thing about learning to keyboard is

   _____

problems and find solutions. Collaboration was an important part of the process. But perhaps the most powerful part of the action research process was the extent to which I became more reflective about what I was doing in the computer lab. The lab at my school has received a lot of praise from administrators, board members, and teachers, and I believe that going through the action research process has had much to do with the continued success of the lab.

I don't look at classroom problems quite the same way now. For example, I also teach middle school choir and began to notice that the weeks on which I saw eighth graders on Mondays (we're on block scheduling), it was usually a difficult, if not unproductive rehearsal. Keeping some informal data about those days and reflecting about why they were so difficult led me to try some interventions that might help alleviate the problem. It may be a bit corny, but action research has changed my life . . . in the classroom anyway.

Student learning is enhanced, I approach problems more systematically, I gather data more carefully and accurately, and my practice is more reflective.

The year following my word processing action research project, I had the good fortune to be a mentor for other teachers learning the action research process. Based on this experience, two observations come to mind. Problem formulation is a difficult process. Extra time spent in this phase of the action research cycle will prevent backtracking, headaches, and frustration down the road. When teachers do identify something that needs addressing, there appears to be a measurable difference between problems that are student centered and those that arise from a teacher complaint about a teaching situation. It appeared that the problems that are student centered are more likely to result in the improvement of instruction.

Making action research a natural part of the teaching process, in the classroom and the school, is critical to success. Traditionally, teachers are not researchers. The school routine isn't geared to provide teachers with the time and resources that research demands. Teachers are considered to be working only when they're in front of a class. On the other hand, teachers need to develop the attitude that improvement of the teaching/learning process can and should be addressed with data-based decision making formalized through action research.

▪▪

THE DECISION about what data are collected for an action research area of focus is largely determined by the nature of the problem. There is no one recipe for how to proceed with data collection efforts. Rather, the individual or group must determine what data will contribute to their understanding and resolution of a given problem. Hence, data collection associated with action research is largely an idiosyncratic approach fueled by the desire to understand one's practice and to collect data that is appropriate and accessible.

The emphasis in this chapter is on qualitative (experience-based) data collection techniques as compared to quantitative (number-based) techniques. Such techniques include data sources such as fieldnotes, journals, surveys, attitude scales, standardized test scores, maps, audiotapes, and videotapes.

One approach is not *better* than the other. However, the literature on action research supports the assertion that qualitative methods are more appropriately applied to action research efforts compared to the application of an experimental pretest, posttest control group design in which the teacher researcher randomly assigns children to a control group or experimental group in order to receive a "treatment." Qualitative research is not the "easy" way out for teacher researchers who fear statistics (a.k.a. sadistics!). As you will see, the rigor of good qualitatively oriented action research equals the rigor of doing good quantitatively oriented action research. If your area of focus necessitates a more quantitative, experimental approach, you should consult more quantitatively oriented references such as Tuckman (1999), and Vockell and Asher (1996).

Qualitative Data Collection Techniques

The receptivity among educators in general, and action researchers specifically, to a qualitative (descriptive) way of examining problems is reflected in the action research literature that emphasizes the following data collection techniques and sources:

- Existing archival sources within a school.
- Tools for capturing everyday life.
- Tools for questioning.
- Conventional sources (surveys, questionnaires, etc.)
- Inventive sources (exhibits, portfolios, etc.).
- Interviews.
- Oral history and narrative stories.
- Rating scales.
- Inventories.
- Observation.
- Mapping.
- Visual recordings.
- Photography.
- Journals and diaries.
  (Sagor, 1992; Calhoun, 1994; Wells, 1994; Anderson et al., 1994; and Stringer, 1996)

As you can see from these examples, the kinds of data you collect would be descriptive, narrative, and even nonwritten forms. In many cases, these data occur naturally and are regularly collected by teachers and administrators. In simple terms, we are engaging in an activity that seeks to answer the question: "What is going on here?" It is not a mysterious quest, but is quite simply an effort to collect data that increases our understanding of the phenomenon under investigation.

In the following sections we will look at the myriad of data collection techniques that can shed light on your area of focus. In research terms, this desire to use multiple sources of data is referred to as **triangulation.**

Triangulation

It is generally accepted in action research circles that researchers should not rely on any single source of data, interview, observation, or instrument. Sagor (1992) has even suggested that action researchers complete a data collection plan that identifies at least three "independent windows for collecting data on the question being investigated" (p. 45). We will adopt a less prescriptive approach here, but we support the triangulation principle. That is, the strength of qualitative research lies in its triangulation, collecting information in many ways rather than relying solely on one (Wolcott, 1988). Pelto and Pelto (1978) have described this as a "multi-instrument" approach (p. 122). For our purposes in doing action research, this suggests that the teacher is the research instrument who, in collecting data, utilizes a variety of techniques over an extended period of time "ferreting out varying perspectives on complex issues and events" (Wolcott, 1988, p. 192). It is important that as we begin to focus our data collection efforts we keep in mind the principle of triangulation and apply it to our regular data collection efforts.

The three primary fieldwork strategies we will discuss in this chapter are experiencing, "enquiring," and examining (Wolcott, 1992, p. 19). Each of these strategies will be discussed in the context of actual teacher researchers' experiences.

Teachers undertaking action research have countless opportunities to observe in their own classrooms. They observe as a normal component of their teaching—monitoring and adjusting instruction based on the verbal and nonverbal interactions in their classrooms. Therefore, using direct observation as a data collection strategy is familiar and not overly time-consuming. As teachers we are constantly observing our environment and adjusting our teaching based on what we see. Action research gives us a systematic and rigorous way to view this process of observation as a qualitative data collection technique.

Participant Observation

The action research vignettes shared at the beginnings of chapters 1, 2, and 3 illustrate how teachers "experience" their teaching through observation. James Rockford observed the "hunt-and-peck" keyboarding strategies of his students as a natural part of his teaching. Cathy Mitchell observed audience reactions to the "Violence Improv" and recorded fieldnotes in her daily journal. Deborah South observed the interpersonal interactions of her "study skills" students and recorded her observations in a journal—observations that quickly confirmed that there were major problems in the classroom. These experiences are all examples of participant observation.

If the researcher is "a genuine participant in the activity being studied," then he or she is called a **participant observer** (McMillan, 1996, p. 245). Participant observation is undertaken with at least two purposes in mind:

- To observe the activities, people, and physical aspects of a situation, and
- To engage in activities that are appropriate to a given situation that provide useful information (Spradley, 1980).

Participant observation can be done to varying degrees depending on the situation being observed and the opportunities presented: A participant observer can be an *active participant observer; a privileged, active observer;* or *a passive observer* (Pelto & Pelto, 1978, Spradley, 1980, and Wolcott, 1982, 1997). Depending on the nature of the problem, teachers have many opportunities to be active participants in the observation process as they go about their work. However, the tendency with observing is to try to see it all! A good rule of thumb here is to try to do less—better. That is, as you embark on some degree of participant observation, do not be overwhelmed with the task. It is not humanly possible to take in everything that you experience. Be content with furthering your understanding of your area of focus through *manageable* observations. Avoid trying to do too much and you will be happier with the outcomes.

Active Participant Observer

Teachers by virtue of teaching are active participant observers of their teaching practice. When actively engaged in teaching, teachers observe the outcomes of their teaching. Each time we teach we monitor the effects of our teaching and adjust our instruction accordingly. As an active participant observer of our own teaching practices, however, we may be so fully immersed in what we are doing that we don't have time to record our observations in a systematic way during the school day. Such recording is a necessary part of being an active participant observer.

In the action research vignettes from chapters 1, 2, and 3, we saw teachers who were active participant observers of their own teaching. Deborah South observed the "off-task" behavior of her "unmotivated" students during the study skills lessons, Cathy Mitchell observed the nature of the audience participation while she directed the teen theater, and James Rockford observed the "hunt-and-peck" strategies used by keyboarding students while he was teaching keyboarding skills. As researchers of our own teaching practices, active participant observation is likely to be the most common "experiencing" data collection technique that we use.

Privileged, Active Observer

There may also be opportunities for teachers to observe in a more privileged, active role. That is, they may wish to observe their children during a time when they are not directly responsible for the teaching of a lesson, for example, during a "specialist's" time in music, library, or physical education. These times provide opportunities for teachers to work as a "teacher's aide" at the same time they can withdraw, stand back, and watch what is happening during a particular teaching episode—moving in and out of the role of teacher, aide, and observer.

Many teachers comment on how valuable these experiences have been in allowing them time to observe the social interactions of students and the impact of a particular instructional strategy on those interactions. By necessity, these privileged, active observer opportunities require teachers to give up valuable time that is often dedicated to duties other than teaching, such as planning, attending team meetings, reading, visiting other classrooms, and relaxing (the all-important "downtime" during a day if they are fortunate enough to have such a schedule). Taking time to observe one's class is a valuable use of nonteaching time that honors a teacher's effort to improve practice, based, in part, on observational data.

Passive Observer

There are also opportunities for teachers to be passive observers in classrooms and schools. When a teacher takes on the role of passive observer, she no longer assumes the responsibilities of the teacher—she should be focused only on her data collection. A privileged, active observer could be turned into being a passive observer by making explicit to the students and a teaching colleague that the classroom teacher is present only to "see what's going on around here." Students will quickly learn that there are times when their teacher is not going to interact with them as she usually does. The teacher might simply announce that today "I am going to watch and learn from what you are doing!" Taking a step back from the daily rigor of being "on-stage" and performing can be refreshing and provide an insightful opportunity for teachers unaccustomed to watching their students in a different setting, through a different lens.

Fieldnotes

The written records of participant observers are often referred to as **fieldnotes**. For teachers undertaking participant observation efforts in their classrooms, these fieldnotes may take the form of anecdotal records compiled as part of a more systematic authentic assessment or portfolio effort. So, what do you write down in these fieldnotes? Well, it depends on what you are looking for! I can offer only limited guidance to help quell your concerns about the "how-to" of writing fieldnotes. But first let me start with an example of how *not* to do fieldnotes!

During my graduate studies at the University of Oregon, I took a class on "Ethnographic Research in Education," and as part of learning how to do ethnography (qualitative research) I was required to conduct a "beginning ethnography" of something that was "culturally different" for me. As an Australian studying in the United States, I had a number of opportunities to study a culturally different phenomenon while at the same time having fun with the project. I chose to study a sorority. As part of this study I participated in one of the regular ceremonies that was part of the sorority members' lives—a formal dinner held each Monday night at which members were required to wear dresses and male guests were expected to wear a jacket and tie.

During the course of the dinner, I frequently excused myself to visit the restroom, stopping along the way to take out my notebook so I could try to record quotes and reconstruct events as they were happening—trying to capture in great detail all that I was observing. Of course, the irony in this strategy was that I was missing a great deal of the dinner by removing myself from the setting in a futile effort to record everything. The ridiculousness of the situation became evident when one of my dinner hosts asked me if I was feeling well or if the meal was to my satisfaction. After all, why did I keep leaving the dinner table?!

The message here for teacher researchers who wish to use fieldnotes as part of their data collection efforts is clear: You can't physically record everything that is happening during an observational episode; nor should you try to. The following options for observing and recording fieldnotes are useful ways to proceed (adapted from Wolcott, 1994).

Observe and Record Everything You Possibly Can

If going into an observation you knew exactly what you wanted to observe, you would find this process to be inefficient. Engaging in an effort to "record everything" will quickly attune you to what is of most interest to you. During these observational periods, you can start with a broad sweep of the classroom and gradually narrow your focus as you get a clearer sense of what is most pressing. You can also decide on your strategies for recording observations. You might choose verbatim conversations, maps and illustrations, photographs, videotape or audiotape recordings, or even writing furiously in the fashion of a principal or university professor undertaking an evaluation! It is a very idiosyncratic activity, but follow one rule: Don't run off to the restroom every five minutes—you *will* miss something! Do try to maintain a running record of what is happening in a format that will be most helpful for you.

For example, in my study of a school district attempting multiple change efforts (see Mills, 1988), I attended the 37th Annual McKenzie School District Teacher Inservice Day. Part of my fieldnotes from this observation were as follows:

8:30 A.M. An announcement is made over the public address system requesting that teachers move into the auditorium and take a seat in preparation for the inservice. As the teachers file into the auditorium the pop song "The Greatest Love of All" is played.

8:41 A.M. The Assistant Superintendent welcomes the teachers to the inservice with the conviction that it is also the "best district with the best teachers." The brief welcome is then followed by the Pledge of Allegiance and the introduction of the new Assistant Superintendent.

8:45 A.M. The Assistant Superintendent introduces the Superintendent as "the Superintendent who cares about kids, cares about teachers, and cares about this district."

The next hour of the inservice is focused on introducing new teachers to the district (there were sixty new appointments) and the presentation of information about how a new focus for the district would be at-risk children.

10:00 A.M. The Superintendent returns to the lyrics of "The Greatest Love of All" and suggests that the message from the song may be suitable as the district's charge: "Everyone is searching for a hero. People need someone to look up to. I never found anyone who fulfilled my needs. . . ." The Superintendent compels the teachers to be the heroes for their students and wishes them a successful school year before closing the inservice.

As you can see from this abbreviated example, there is nothing mystical about fieldnotes. They serve as a record of what an observer attended to during the course of an observation and help guide subsequent observations and interviews. This was the beginning of my year-long fieldwork in the McKenzie School District, and this initial observation helped me to frame questions that guided my efforts to understand how central office personnel, principals, and teachers manage and cope with multiple innovations.

Observe and Look for Nothing in Particular

Try to see the routine in new ways. If you can, try to look with "new eyes" and approach the scene as if you were an outsider. Wolcott offers helpful advice for teachers conducting observations in classrooms that are so familiar that everything seems ordinary and routine:

Aware of being familiar with classroom routines, an experienced observer might initiate a new set of observations with the strategy that in yet another classroom one simply assumes "business as usual" . . . The observer sets a sort or radar, scanning constantly for whatever it is that those in the setting are doing to keep the system operating smoothly. (1994, p. 162)

Look for "Bumps" or Paradoxes

In this strategy you consider the environment you are observing as if it were "flat"; nothing in particular stands out to you. It is an opportunity for observers to look for the "bumps" in the setting. In action research projects these "bumps" might be unexpected student responses to a new curriculum or teaching strategy or an unexpected response to a new classroom management plan, seating arrangement, monitoring strategy, or innovation.

For example, the "bumps" observed by a teacher concerned with gender inequity may become painfully evident when the "locus of control" in a classroom is on one or two boys. That is, by keeping a tally of who commanded most of the teacher's attention by answering and asking questions, it became clear that one or two dominant boys were the focus of the activity during a lesson.

This strategy also suggests that teacher researchers look for contradictions or paradoxes in their classrooms. In a sense, this is not dissimilar to the "looking for bumps" strategy, for a paradox will often stand out in an obvious way to the teacher who has taken the time to stand back and look at what is happening in the classroom. (See Key Concept Box 3-1 for a description of the components of effective observation.)

KEY CONCEPTS BOX 3-1

Components of Effective Observation	
PRINCIPAL COMPONENTS	
DEGREES OF PARTICIPATION:	
Participant observer	Engage in activities Observe activities, people, and physical aspects
Privileged observer	A teacher's aide during specialists' time
Passive observer	Present only to observe what's going on
FIELDNOTES:	
Observe and record everything	Attune to what you actually record through verbatim conversations, maps and illustrations, photos, video, and audio recordings.
Observe and look for nothing	Try to see beyond the routine and look with a fresh perspective
Look for paradoxes	What are the unintended consequences of action

For example, teacher researchers often comment on the unintended conse-quences of a particular teaching strategy or a curriculum change that has become evident only when they have had an opportunity to stand back and observe the results of their actions. These consequences often present themselves in the form of a paradox—a contradiction in terms. For example, as one teacher researcher commented after attempting to incorporate manipulatives into her math instruc-tion in a primary classroom, "I thought that the use of manipulatives in teaching mathematics would also lead to increased cooperation in group work. Instead, what I saw were my kids fighting over who got to use what and not wanting to share."

Enquiring: When the Researcher Asks

A second major category of data collection techniques can be grouped as data that are collected by the teacher through the asking of questions. Teacher researchers may ask questions of students, parents, and other teachers using **interviewing** and **questionnaire** techniques.

As Michael Agar (1980) suggests, information from interviews can serve as the "methodological core" against which observational data can be used to "feed" ongoing informal interviews. That is, observational data (collected through the "experiencing" techniques described earlier) can suggest questions that can be asked in subsequent interviews with children, parents, teachers—whomever the participants in the study might be. Participants in an interview may possibly leave things out. Pairing observation and interviewing provides a valuable way to gather complementary data. For example, Cathy Mitchell's Teen Theater Group (see chapter 2) developed a group interview technique based on observations of audience reactions to performances. This technique involved three company members meeting with a small group of audience members for about fifteen minutes following a performance so that they could gauge the audience response to the scenes about teen violence and harassment. One actor served as the in-terviewer, one as the scribe, and one kept a running tally of comments and responses.

Informal Ethnographic Interview

The **informal ethnographic interview** is little more than a casual conversation that allows the teacher, in a conversational style, to inquire into something that has presented itself as an opportunity to learn about their practice. Agar (1980) sug-gests strategies that allow teacher researchers to have a ready set of questions to ask participants in a study, for example, the "5 Ws and H": *who, what, where, when, why,* and *how.* Using these prompts, teachers will never be at a loss for a question to add to their understanding of what is happening in their classrooms. For example, in considering the example of the teacher researching the impact of manipulatives on math performance, and through observation recognizing the unanticipated consequence of poor sharing of manipulatives, the teacher might ask questions such as these:

- *Who* should be responsible for rotating the materials through the group?
- *What* was the cause of the problem?
- *Where* did the problem originate?
- *When* did the problem of sharing begin?
- *Why* don't you want to share the manipulatives with each other?
- *How* do you think we can solve this problem?

Following the episode, the teacher might briefly jot down in a plan book a summary of what the students had to say and refer back to it later as a valuable data source. Alternatively, the teacher researcher may keep anecdotal records on each student and simply make an entry on the student's file. An example of a student anecdotal record form is presented in Figure 3–1.

Structured Formal Interviews

Teacher researchers may also want to consider formally interviewing children, parents, or colleagues as part of their data collection efforts. Using a structured interview format allows the teacher to ask all of the participants the same series of questions. However, a major challenge in constructing any interview is to phrase questions in such a way that they elicit the information you really want. While this may seem obvious, teacher researchers often feel compelled by tradition and history to ask a lengthy set of questions of which only a part is really their focus. When planning interviews, consider the following options for ensuring the quality of your structured formal interviews:

- **Pilot questions on a similar group of respondents.** That is, if you have developed an interview schedule to use with the students in your classroom, try it out on some similarly aged students (not in your class) to see if it makes sense. Their feedback will quickly confirm, or challenge, the assumptions you have made about appropriate language. Using the feedback from the students, revise the questionnaire before administering it to your children.
- **Use questions that vary from convergent to divergent.** That is, use both "open-ended" and "closed" questions in a structured interview or questionnaire. For example, a closed (convergent) question allows for a brief response such as "Yes/No." Alternatively, an open-ended (divergent) question can conclude with an "Other comments" section, or a request for the interviewee to "add anything else" they would like to. In so doing, you will provide students with opportunities to elaborate on questions in ways that you had never anticipated. It should also be noted, however, that the information gathered through open-ended questions is often more difficult to make sense of. But it does allow the teacher researcher to obtain information that might otherwise be considered "outlying" or "discrepant."
- **Persevere with silence and "wait time" to elicit a response.** Otherwise it becomes too easy to answer your own question! (The components of interviewing are listed in Key Concepts Box 3–2.)

FIGURE 3–1 Student Anecdotal Record Form

Student Anecdotal Record Form

Name: _Mary Smith_

Grade _K_

Date: _10/23_   Comments: _Writing table_
observation. Mary appears unhappy during the time
she spends at the writing table. Her explanation:
"I don't have time to think about my story."

Date: _____   Comments: _____

KEY CONCEPTS BOX 3–2

Components of Interviewing	
Informal interviews	5 Ws and H *who, what, where, when, why,* and *how*?
Structured formal interviews	Pilot the interview. Use a variety of question formats. Use divergent and convergent questions. Allow ample "wait time" to elicit a response.

Questionnaires

Perhaps the major difference between a structured interview schedule and a questionnaire is that the student or parent will write out the responses on the form provided. Clearly there are positives and negatives with each approach: questionnaires allow the teacher researcher to collect large amounts of data in a relatively short amount of time (compared to interviewing the same number of students or parents), while interviews allow an opportunity for the teacher to intimately know how each student (and parent) feels about a particular issue, but in a time-consuming fashion that few teacher researchers feel is justified. A compromise is to use a questionnaire (when appropriate) and to conduct follow-up interviews with students who have provided written feedback that warrants further investigation. For example, in a conversational way, teachers as part of their regular teaching may ask, "Mary, in the questionnaire you returned you commented that. . . . Can you tell me a little more about that?" Similarly, as part of a parent-teacher conference the teacher may follow up with parents who have returned questionnaires.

Clearly, there is one major assumption associated with the use of a questionnaire—the student can read and write. Many teacher researchers exclude the use of a questionnaire on this basis alone, but also compromise the time it takes to interview all of their students by interviewing only a "representative sample" in their class.

A solid data collection instrument will help ensure useful responses. Consider the following guidelines for developing and presenting questionnaires:

1. **Carefully proofread questionnaires** (or better still have a "critical" friend read your questionnaire) before sending them out. Nothing will turn parents off quicker than receiving a message from their child's teacher that is littered with errors. Alternatively, students may be thrilled by the chance to point out that there is an error in their teacher's written work.

2. **Avoid a sloppy presentation.** Make the survey attractive and consider using BIG print if necessary.

3. **Avoid a lengthy questionnaire.** Piloting the instrument will give you a realistic sense of how long it will take for your students (or parents) to complete the task. Remember, no matter how much they want to help you, if it's too long it will find its way into the "circular file" instead of back into your hands.

4. **Do not ask unnecessary questions.** This is akin to teachers developing tests that don't match what was taught—a common complaint directed toward the administration of standardized tests. Often, we feel compelled to ask a great deal of trivial information on a questionnaire that is tangential to our stated purpose.

5. **Use structured items with a variety of possible responses.** (See the discussion of Likert Scales in this chapter.) Indicate what you mean by "often" and "frequently" and how they differ from each other. Otherwise, your respondents will interpret the meaning of the terms in quite different ways.

6. **Whenever possible, allow for an "Other Comments" section.** This provides respondents with an opportunity to respond openly to your questions. These comments also provide you with an excellent source of "discrepant"

	Keys to Questionnaires

_____ Proofread the questionnaire carefully.

_____ Avoid a sloppy presentation.

_____ Avoid a lengthy questionnaire.

_____ Do not ask unnecessary questions.

_____ Use structured items with a variety of possible responses.

_____ Include an "Other Comments" section.

_____ Decide whether to use respondents' names.

_____ Pilot the questionnaire.

_____ Use a variety of question formats.

data ("I hadn't expected someone to say that!") and an opportunity to follow up with an informal interview to elicit more information from the respondent as your time, energy, and inquisitiveness allow. For example, "In your response to question #3 you stated that. . . . Can you tell me a little more about what you meant?"

7. **Decide whether you want respondents to put their names on the questionnaires or whether you will use a number to keep track of who has responded.** You should assure respondents (students, parents, colleagues) that their confidentiality will be protected throughout the process. However, you can protect respondents while also keeping track of who has responded and deciding whether they have made comments that you feel warrant a follow-up conversation. The key issue here is to assure the students, parents, and colleagues that they will not suffer any negative consequences for anything they might share with you. If we want respondents to be honest and forthright in their answers, we must assure them that they will not be persecuted if they tell us something we don't want to read or hear. (For further discussion of this matter see the section on ethics at the end of chapter 4). (See Research in Action Checklist 3–1 for guidelines on devising a questionnaire.)

Attitude Scales

Many teacher researchers are curious about the impact of their work on students' attitudes. Scales that are often used to measure attitudes, such as Likert scales and semantic differentials, are useful tools for the action researcher. The use of attitude scales allows teacher researchers to determine "what an individual believes, perceives, or feels" (Gay, 1996, p. 155). Nearly all of the action research vignettes in this book include examples of how teacher researchers wanted to know how children "felt" about something (a keyboarding software program, the violence and harassment scenes presented by the Teen Theater group, the absenteeism policy at the school, and the deemphasis of grades). In some cases these teacher researchers used an attitude scale, whereas others used open-ended questions such as "How do you feel about the school's absenteeism policy?"

Likert Scales

A **Likert scale** asks students to respond to a series of statements indicating whether they strongly agree (SA), agree (A), are undecided (U), disagree (D), or strongly disagree (SD) with each statement. Each response corresponds with a point value and a score is determined by adding the point values for each statement. For example, the following point values might be assigned for positive responses: SA = 5, A = 4, U = 3, D = 2, SD = 1. As Gay (1996) points out, "A high point value on a positively stated item would indicate a positive attitude and a high total score on the test would be indicative of a positive attitude" (p. 155).

While these instruments provide teacher researchers with quantitative (numerical) data, these data can still be considered descriptive. While the responses to such a survey can be reduced to numbers (for example, the average response was 4.2), the data are still largely descriptive and analyzed using descriptive statistics such as mean and standard deviation (see chapter 5) and an accompanying narrative. (For example, the average response was 4.2 and was supported by the following comments. . . .)

To illustrate, students experiencing a new math curriculum that emphasizes problem-solving strategies may be asked to respond to the following item on a questionnaire:

> Please respond to the following items by drawing a circle around the response that most closely reflects your opinion; strongly agree (SA), agree (A), undecided (U), disagree (D), or strongly disagree (SD).
>
> 1. I believe that the problem-solving skills I learn in class help me make good problem-solving decisions outside of school.
>
> SA   A   U   D   SD

By assigning the following point values, SA = 5, A = 4, U = 3, D = 2, SD = 1, the teacher researcher would be able to infer whether the students felt positively or negatively about the effect of math problem-solving skills outside of the classroom.

Semantic Differential

A **semantic differential** asks a student (or parent) to give a quantitative rating to the subject of the rating scale on a number of bipolar adjectives. For example, following the implementation of a new math curriculum, students might be asked to rate the curriculum in terms of whether it was exciting or boring, relevant or irrelevant, or enjoyable or unenjoyable.

Each location on the continuum between the bipolar words has an associated score:

$$\text{Boring} \underline{\quad}\underline{\quad}\underline{\quad}\underline{\quad}\underline{\quad}\underline{\quad}\underline{\quad} \text{Exciting}$$
$$-3\ -2\ -1\ \ \ 0\ \ \ 1\ \ \ 2\ \ \ 3$$

$$\text{Irrelevant} \underline{\quad}\underline{\quad}\underline{\quad}\underline{\quad}\underline{\quad}\underline{\quad}\underline{\quad} \text{Relevant}$$
$$-3\ -2\ -1\ \ \ 0\ \ \ 1\ \ \ 2\ \ \ 3$$

$$\text{Unenjoyable} \underline{\quad}\underline{\quad}\underline{\quad}\underline{\quad}\underline{\quad}\underline{\quad}\underline{\quad} \text{Enjoyable}$$
$$-3\ -2\ -1\ \ \ 0\ \ \ 1\ \ \ 2\ \ \ 3$$

By totaling scores for all items on the semantic differential, the teacher researcher can determine whether a child's attitude is positive or negative. Semantic differential scales usually have five to seven intervals with a neutral attitude being assigned a value of zero.

A child who checked the first interval on each of these items would be expressing a positive attitude toward mathematics (for further discussion of semantic differentials see Gay, 1996 and Pelto & Pelto, 1978).

Other Measurement Techniques

Teacher researchers are often pressured or required to use standardized tests. It is not possible to list here all of the standardized tests that exist. We should acknowledge, however, that standardized test scores are another data source that contributes to our understanding of how teaching practices affect our students. A good source for teachers who are investigating standardized tests is the Mental Measurements Yearbooks (MMYs), which provide a sometimes bewildering array of test information used by researchers and teachers alike. This encyclopedia of test descriptions and reviews should satisfy most quests to find an appropriate test. Alternatively, teacher researchers can contact their local school districts to check out available tests or get names of contacts at the state level to identify an appropriate test.

Examining: Using and Making Records

This third category for data collection techniques suggests a "catch-all" term to describe everything else that a teacher researcher may collect. Again, many of these data sources are naturally occurring and require only that the teacher locate them within their school setting.

Archival Documents

Like classrooms, schools are repositories for all sorts of records—student records, minutes of meetings (faculty, PTA, school board), newspaper clippings about significant events in the community, and so on. With permission, the teacher researcher can use these sources of data to gain valuable historical insights, identify potential trends, and explain how things got to be the way they are. Clearly, there are many archival data sources that can be accessed by teacher researchers if indicated by their focus areas. Often, clerical assistants, school aids, and student teachers are happy to help with uncovering archival data and organizing it in a way that is most useful to the classroom teacher if they believe that it is contributing to the collective understanding of a pressing educational issue. Don't be bashful about asking for assistance with this task.

Some of the many archival data sources that exist in schools include the following:

- Attendance rates.
- Retention rates.
- Discipline referrals.
- Dropout rates.
- Suspension rates.
- Attendance rates at parent-teacher conferences.
- Disaggregated data by grade level for student performance on statewide assessments in math, reading, writing, etc.
- Standardized test scores.
- Student participation rates in extracurricular activities. (Calhoun, 1994)

Journals

Daily journals kept by students and teachers alike are also a valuable data source. As Anderson, Herr, and Nihlen (1994) point out:

> The journal acts as a narrative technique and records events, thoughts, and feelings that have importance for the writer. As a record kept by a student, it can inform the teacher researcher about changing thoughts and new ideas and the progression of learning. (p. 153)

Students' journals can provide teachers with a valuable window into the students' world (in much the same way that homework assignments provide parents with insights into their children's daily experiences). A daily journal kept by teachers can also be an opportunity to keep a narrative account of their perspectives of what is happening in their classrooms.

Cochran-Smith and Lytle (1993) have incorporated teachers' journals as a central part of their work with teacher researchers and offer a somewhat expanded definition of what journals might incorporate:

- Journals are records of classroom life in which teachers write observations, and reflect on their teaching over time.
- Journals are a collection of descriptions, analyses, and interpretations.
- Journals capture the essence of what is happening with students in classrooms and what this means for future teaching episodes.

- Journals provide teachers with a way to revisit, analyze, and evaluate their experiences over time.
- Journals provide windows on what goes on in school through teachers' eyes. (Cochran-Smith & Lytle, 1993, pp. 26–27).

Journals, conceptualized in this way, are more than a single data source—they are an ongoing attempt by teachers to systematically reflect on their practice by constructing a narrative that honors the unique and powerful voice of the teachers' language. Regardless of your specific area of focus, journaling is recommended as a way to keep track of not only observations but feelings associated with the action research process.

Making Maps, Video- and Audiotapes, Photographs, Film, and Artifacts

These nonwritten sources of data can also be extremely helpful for teacher researchers trying to monitor movements in a classroom—data that are not always easily recorded in a narrative form.

Construction of Maps

Teacher researchers find class maps and school maps useful for a number of reasons. They provide contextual insights for people who have not visited the school, and they provide the teacher researcher with a reflective tool—a way of rethinking the way things are in their classrooms. For example, why are the computers in the classroom placed in a "bank" along one wall, and what are the effects of the individual student computer time on other seat-work activities? A map can also record traffic flow in a classroom as well as teacher movement during instruction.

The school map may also prove useful for teams of teachers concerned about the movement and interactions of different grade levels of students and any problems that emerge from the traffic flow. Quite simply, maps are an easy, useful tool that help teacher researchers and the people with whom they are sharing their research locate particular teaching episodes in the space of the teacher's classroom or school. For qualitatively oriented classroom researchers, context is everything! Figure 3–2 shows an example of a classroom map.

Use of Videotape, Audiotape, Photographs, and Film

Videotapes and audiotapes provide teacher researchers with another data source when the teacher is fully engaged in teaching but still wants to capture classroom events and interactions. Of course, there are downsides to these techniques. For example, their presence may elicit the usual "funny faces" and bizarre comments that we normally associate with the presence of such technology in a classroom for the first time. One way of moving ahead with these efforts is to introduce them into a classroom early in an action research project and provide the illusion that the "camera is running" when, in fact, there is no film in the camera. Alternatively, be prepared to use a lot of videotape and audiotape and record over them! However, with the move to outcome-based performance assessment and "capstone" experiences, children are often required to demonstrate knowledge and skills through presentations to peers or panels of teachers and parents. Videotape is an

FIGURE 3–2 Classroom Map Example

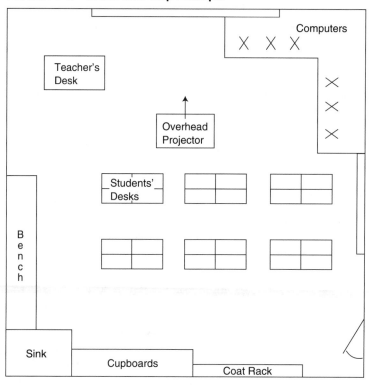

excellent way to capture these events and to provide an opportunity for teachers and students alike to reflect on content, skills, and attitudes demonstrated by the students.

Assuming there are no technical problems (and that is a pretty big assumption!), the use of audiotape and videotape also raises the serious issue of time—the time it takes to watch, listen, and record observations from these recorded sources. While finding enough time has the potential to be the number one challenge for teachers doing action research, it is important for us to weigh the potential benefits and drawbacks of these data sources. These techniques have the potential to be more time-consuming and hence potentially threatening to the goodwill of any action research endeavor. However, many teacher researchers use these methods to great advantage—which only confirms the idiosyncratic nature of data collection efforts!

Artifacts

Classrooms are rich sources of what we might call **artifacts**—written or visual sources of data that contribute to our understanding of what is happening in our classrooms and schools. The category of artifact can include almost everything else that we haven't already discussed. For example, there has been a trend in schools to move toward "authentic assessment" techniques, including the use of student

Components of Using and Making Records	
Archival sources	Minutes of meetings Attendance rates, retention rates, dropout rates, suspension rates Discipline referrals Statewide assessment scores Newspaper clippings
Journals	Daily observations and analysis Reflections Record keeping
Artifacts	Maps and seating charts Photographs, audio- and videotapes Portfolios or less formal examples of student work

portfolios—a presentation of work that captures individual student's work samples over time and the relative growth of that work. Portfolios, while difficult to quantify, provide the teacher with valuable outcome data that gets at the heart of the qualitatively different samples of work. Such artifacts are a valuable data source that teachers may use as a starting point for conversation with their students. Key Concepts Box 3–3 shows the components of using and making records.

Hence, we have gone full circle in looking at how teacher researchers could use the contents of student portfolios as the basis for an informal interview with their students as they search for greater understanding of the students' perspectives of their learning. For example, a teacher may ask a student to elaborate on the thinking behind a piece of creative writing, artwork, or explanation of an open-ended mathematics problem-solving solution. Utilize Agar's "5Ws and H" to informally engage students in conversation about their work—you'll be pleased with the outcome and the return for your investment of time. Key Concepts Box 3–4 shows the taxonomy of action research qualitative data collection techniques.

Realign Your Area of Focus and Action Research Plan When Necessary

By this point in the action research process, teacher researchers have already articulated their area of focus in a problem statement and reviewed the literature based on that idea. However, once they start their data collection, many teacher researchers find themselves drawn into other directions that appear more interesting, relevant, or problematic. That is the very nature of action research; it is intimate, open-ended, and often serendipitous. Being clear about a problem is critical in the beginning, but once teacher researchers begin to systematically collect their data, the area of focus will become even clearer.

Be prepared to modify and adjust your action research plan if necessary. For example, a group of teachers started their action research project with an area of focus on the impact of early literacy development on problem-solving skills in

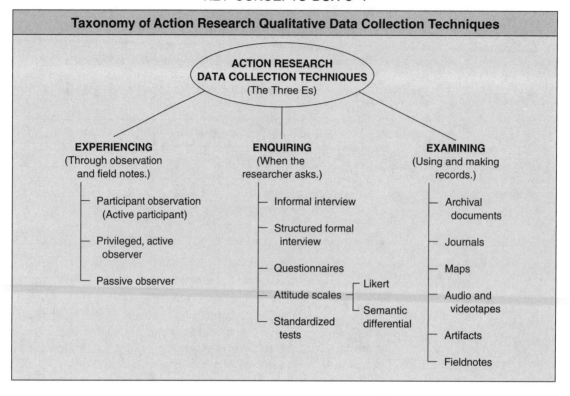

Taxonomy of Action Research Qualitative Data Collection Techniques

ACTION RESEARCH
DATA COLLECTION TECHNIQUES
(The Three Es)

EXPERIENCING
(Through observation
and field notes.)

- Participant observation
  (Active participant)

- Privileged, active
  observer

- Passive observer

ENQUIRING
(When the
researcher asks.)

- Informal interview

- Structured formal
  interview

- Questionnaires

- Attitude scales
  - Likert
  - Semantic
    differential

- Standardized
  tests

EXAMINING
(Using and making
records.)

- Archival
  documents

- Journals

- Maps

- Audio and
  videotapes

- Artifacts

- Fieldnotes

mathematics. As their study evolved, it became clear to the participants that their real focus was not on the transfer of literacy to problem-solving but rather on the effects of a phonemic skills curriculum on early literacy development. When this focus became clear after some initial data collection, the group decided to change their research questions to more accurately reflect the real nature of their work.

There is nothing wrong with realigning your inquiry midway through it. Remember, action research is done to benefit you and the students in your class-room. The process is a spiral. If you discover a question or a method that seems more fruitful than the one you are currently using, adjust your action research plan and continue on!

Summary

This chapter has examined how to identify and develop data collection techniques appropriate for an action research project. The concept of triangulation, or ensuring that teacher researchers do not rely on a single data source, was presented as a guiding principle when thinking about a "multi-instrument" approach to system-atic action research.

Teacher researchers can become participant observers and gather fieldnotes, assuming different degrees of involvement in the class. They can use a variety of inquiry tools such as interviews, questionnaires, or attitude scales to gather data. Teacher researchers can also benefit from the exploration of new or existing school archives and student artifacts.

As you gather data, you may find a more interesting or fruitful line of inquiry. Do not be afraid to revise your action research plan midway to suit your needs.

For Further Thought

1. What data collection techniques will you use to answer each of your research questions?
2. What data collection instruments do you need to locate or develop?

CHAPTER 4

Data Collection Considerations: Validity, Reliability, Generalizability, and Ethics

This chapter addresses the importance of validity, reliability, and generalizability as ways to assure the quality of qualitatively oriented action research. In addition, the chapter describes the ethical issues that confront teacher researchers and suggests a series of ethical guideposts to help ensure that your research is undertaken in an ethical manner.

———

After reading this chapter you should be able to

1. Understand the concepts of validity, reliability, and generalizability as they apply to action research.
2. Clarify ethical issues involved in conducting action research.

The Use of Technology to Enhance Mathematics Achievement

CLEM ANNICE

Children learn at an early age the concept of light refraction. Peering into fishbowls, children see that the fish, rocks, plants, and toys appear larger than life, their movement, shape, and size distorted by the refraction of light. We have all been puzzled at some time in our lives by this illusion and the contradiction between what we see and what we get as we attempt to reach in and touch the inhabitants of the fishbowl. Can the same be said for the use of technology in mathematics reform? Is what we see in classrooms really what we get? Are students and teachers developing a functional and appropriate use of the technology, or are they just playing at the computer? Are teachers and students making connections between the use of technology for presenting models and the concepts that the models represent? How is the use of technology to enhance curriculum and instruction in mathematics affecting student outcomes in mathematics? It is this final question that drove the schoolwide action research project at Billabong Elementary School.

Billabong Elementary School is a large kindergarten to grade 7 school that has embraced the use of technology as a key component of its mathematics curriculum reform efforts. Visitors to the school—and there are many—are given tours. The teachers at Billabong Elementary consider that they "teach in a fishbowl," constantly on display to the outside world. In many ways, the school looks different from traditional schools, and visitors to the school are invited to look into classrooms through the large windows that provide them with snapshots into the inner sanctum of our classrooms.

The principal of Billabong Elementary is described by his teachers as a "visionary leader," and the school has a large collection of computer hardware and software because of the principal's grantwriting efforts. One key component of the principal's vision has been the introduction of technology to the school. In large part, this technology has been made possible through school-business partnerships that he has forged. The principal is committed to the use of technology at Billabong because of what he sees as the gap between the "real world" and the "school world"; he thinks that one way to bridge this gap is to embrace technology in an effort to prepare children for the 21st century.

As a site council responsible for guiding staff development efforts in the school, we decided to focus on the impact of our extensive investment in technology on student achievement in mathematics. In particular, we wanted to know

1. If our use of technology was successfully meeting the National Council of Teachers of Mathematics (NCTM) Standards and
2. How those Standards were being interpreted into classroom practice and student outcomes.

Our action research team decided that we would collect data by observing in each other's classrooms, interviewing teachers and children, analyzing mathematics test data, and comparing the mathematics curriculum taught in the school with the NCTM Standards. When we presented our project to the faculty, all of the teachers and the principal appeared to want to cooperate with the research team's requests for access to classrooms, curriculum materials, and so on. Our hope was to learn more about our technology intervention and how we might continue to evolve as a faculty in this area.

As you move through the halls at Billabong, there is a great deal to be seen—classrooms are open for the inquiring eye. Kindergarten through third-grade classrooms characteristically have six computers, as well as scanners, color printers, and networking with the school's library (thus having access to the extensive CD-ROM collection). The fourth- through seventh-grade classrooms have all of these resources and another six computers per classroom. In one class, all of the children are given an individual laptop computer to use for the year. Children can be seen using computers as part of their class assignments, busying themselves with creating hypercard stacks for creative writing, "playing" math games, and so on. Math learning centers are evident, and each child is given varied opportunities to interact with a number of different math manipulatives: base ten blocks, place value charts, construction materials, colored chips, tangrams, and geo-boards, to name a few.

However, what we saw from the inside of each other's classrooms, was distinctly different from what we had seen from the outside "looking in." For example, in many of the classrooms children could be seen busily engaged with the computers playing math mazes. For the most part, however, children were engaged in low-level activities, and the purpose of the tasks was lost. Many of the children were engaged in "drill-and-kill" activities that had little relevance to their math learning. The computers had taken on the role of an electronic work sheet to keep children busy once they had completed other assigned math tasks.

Interviews with children were revealing. When we interviewed the children, we did so with a guarantee that their responses would be confidential and asked that they be honest with us—after all, our goal was to provide the best possible mathematics learning environment for them that we possibly could. Some children were brutally honest, telling in great detail the kinds of math activities some teachers used on the computers. Some activities were singled out by children as being a "waste of time," and others described some teachers as "not having a clue" about how the computers were really being used. Indeed, some of this information was confirmed by our own observations of classrooms where children had become proficient at "scribbling" on the computer screen using the mouse and a graphics program and quickly returning to the "drill-and-kill" screen when the teacher approached.

While the computers were being heavily used, the appropriateness of their use was questionable. This was no more evident than in classrooms where the calculator function had been removed from the computers. As one teacher explained, "The children are unable to mentally compute, and their basic skills have deteriorated . . . so we can't have them using calculators until they master the basic skills!" There appeared to be consensus among the teachers that there was a direct relationship between providing children with access to computers and children's lack of ability to recall basic math facts.

The interviews with teachers revealed other problems. Many of the teachers knew very little about the NCTM Standards and continued to use their old "tried and proven" curriculum, in spite of a new textbook adoption promoted by the principal. In fact, some teachers were very unhappy about the textbook adoption because no teachers had been consulted in the process—the textbook had been selected by the principal who was a good friend of the author. In return for piloting the curriculum materials in the school, the principal secured free copies of the textbook.

Compared to other schools in the district, our children appeared to be doing below average on statewide assessments. This came as quite a surprise to some teachers who felt that their children were doing well in most math strands with the exception of open-ended problem-solving and algebraic relationships. In these teachers' views the problem was with the appropriateness of the tests, not the use of technology to enhance teaching and learning.

The findings of our schoolwide action research effort raised some difficult ethical dilemmas for the action research team:

1. What do we do with the data that provided a negative picture of individual teachers in the school? Do we share data on an individual basis with teachers who were singled out by students? What risks do we run in sharing this information? How can we promote professional development without hurting anyone?

2. What do we do with the data that indicated a great deal of dissatisfaction with how the principal had mandated the choice of curriculum? Do we risk alienating the teachers from the administration? Could some teachers be hurt professionally by action the principal might take?
3. How can we improve student achievement through the use of technology without hurting teachers (and the principal) in the process?

The action research team decided to adopt a "hold harmless" approach to dealing with the findings of the study. We shared the general findings of the study with teachers at a faculty meeting and invited teachers, on a voluntary basis, to meet with us to discuss the data for their classrooms. Similarly, we invited the principal to meet with us to discuss implications of the findings for future professional development opportunities.

ATTENTION TO THE three important concepts of validity, reliability, and generalizability will help teacher researchers ensure the quality of their work. These concepts are also important for teacher researchers who are reviewing published and unpublished research. That is, to both do action research and measure the quality of the action research you're reading about, you need a basic understanding of the concepts of validity, reliability, and generalizability.

Qualitative researchers, action researchers, and quantitative researchers disagree about the value of applying these concepts of validity, reliability, and generalizability to qualitatively oriented action research. In part, this debate takes place because such concepts have their roots in traditional quantitative research—research that uses mostly numerical data and that has different purposes from action research (see chapter 1).

However, it is important for teacher researchers to understand the meanings of these terms to be knowledgeable consumers of research, as well as producers of research that we hope will be trustworthy and persuasive in their own eyes and in the eyes of their audience.

Validity

The use of the word *validity* is common in our everyday professional language. For example, teachers will ask, "Are the results of the California Achievement Test really valid?" Or, my preservice teachers will often comment, "My students did poorly on the history test I gave them, but I'm not sure it's an accurate representation of what they really know." Recently, I have also heard teachers discuss whether open-ended assessment strategies really measure their students' ability. All of these examples are questions about **validity**, or how we know that the data we collect (test scores, for example) accurately gauge what we are trying to measure (in this case, what it is that our children "know" about history). To put it technically, "validity refers to the degree to which scientific observations actually measure or record what they purport to measure" (Pelto & Pelto, 1978, p. 33).

Historically, validity was linked to numerically based research conducted in the positivistic tradition. For example, Chronbach and Meehl (1955) developed criteria for four different types of validity. All of these types of validity served the purpose of convincing the researcher and the researched that the "results" of the research were "right," "accurate," and could withstand scrutiny from other researchers.

However, as many types of qualitative research became more popular in classroom settings in the late 1970s and early 1980s, it became common for qualitative researchers to begin to justify and defend the validity of their studies according to the criteria that had previously been applied to quantitative studies. For example, as a graduate student completing a research-based masters thesis on the effects of high geographic mobility on the children of low-income families, I was required by my advisors to dedicate considerable time and effort to justifying and defending the accuracy of my account. They confronted me with the question, "How will your readers know that your case studies accurately portray the lives of these children?" (Mills, 1985).

In the early days of my career this seemed like an overwhelming task, for there was a general dearth of literature that specifically dealt with the issue. Since then, individuals have been experimenting with a new vocabulary that captures the essence of the term *validity* in a way that applies specifically to the methods of qualitative research. Kincheloe asks "Is *trustworthiness* a more appropriate word to use?" (1991, p. 135), whereas Wolcott suggests "*understanding* seems to encapsulate the idea as well as any other everyday term" (1994, p. 367).

Let's look at two systems for measuring the quality of qualitative research based on these two terms: trustworthiness and understanding.

Guba's Criteria for Validity of Qualitative Research

Egon Guba's article "Criteria for Assessing the Trustworthiness of Naturalistic Inquiries" (1981) speaks directly to qualitative researchers. Guba argued that the **trustworthiness** of qualitative inquiry could be established by addressing the following characteristics of a study: *credibility, transferability, dependability,* and *confirmability.*

Credibility

The **credibility** of the study refers to the researcher's ability to take into account all of the complexities that present themselves in a study and to deal with patterns that are not easily explained. To do this, Guba suggested that the following methods be used:

- *Do prolonged participation at the study site* to overcome distortions produced by the presence of researchers and to provide researchers with the opportunity to test biases and perceptions. By virtue of studying your own school, classroom, and students, you will be immersed in the setting and spend a prolonged amount of time at the site—probably close to 180 days a year!
- *Do persistent observation* to identify pervasive qualities as well as atypical characteristics.
- *Do peer debriefing* to provide researchers with the opportunity to test their growing insights through interactions with other professionals. For example, most of us will be able to identify a "critical friend," a colleague, "significant

other," somebody who is willing and able to help us reflect on own situations by listening, prompting, and recording our insights throughout the process.

- *Practice triangulation* (discussed in chapter 3) to compare a variety of data sources and different methods with one another in order to cross-check data.
- *Collect documents, films, videotapes, audio recordings, artifacts, and other "raw" or "slice-of-life" data items.*
- *Do member checks* to test the overall report with the study's participants before sharing it in final form (Guba, 1981, pp. 84–86).
- *Establish structural corroboration or coherence* to ensure that there are no internal conflicts or contradictions.
- *Establish referential adequacy*, that is, to test analyses and interpretations against documents, recordings, films, and the like that were collected as part of the study.

Transferability

Guba's second criteria of **transferability** refers to qualitative researchers' beliefs that everything they study is context bound and that the goal of their work is not to develop "truth" statements that can be generalized to larger groups of people. To facilitate the development of descriptive, context-relevant statements, Guba proposed that the researcher should:

- *Collect detailed descriptive* data that will permit comparison of a given context (classroom/school) to other possible contexts to which transfer might be contemplated.
- *Develop detailed descriptions of the context* to make judgments about fittingness with other contexts possible. (Guba, 1981)

The transferability of an action research account depends largely on whether the consumer of the research can identify with the setting. Include as much detail as possible to allow the recipients of your work to "see" the setting for themselves.

Dependability

According to Guba, **dependability** refers to the stability of the data. To address issues related to the dependability of the data we collect, Guba recommended the following steps:

- *Overlap methods* (similar to a triangulation process). Use two or more methods in such a way that the weakness of one is compensated by the strength of another. For example, interviews with students may be used to contribute to our understanding of what we observed happening during a lesson.
- *Establish an "audit trail."* This process makes it possible for an external "auditor" (maybe a critical friend, principal, or graduate student) to examine the processes of data collection, analysis, and interpretation (Guba, 1981). This audit trail may take the form of a written description of each process and perhaps even access to original fieldnotes, artifacts, videotapes, pictures, archival data, and so on.

Confirmability

The final characteristic that Guba addresses is the **confirmability** of the data, or the neutrality or objectivity of the data that has been collected. Guba argues that the following two steps can be taken to address this issue:

- *Practice triangulation,* (discussed in chapter 3) whereby a variety of data sources and different methods are compared with one another to cross-check data.
- *Practice reflexivity,* that is, to intentionally reveal underlying assumptions or biases that cause the researcher to formulate a set of questions in a particular way and to present findings in a particular way. One technique for doing this is to keep a journal in which reflections/musings are recorded on a regular basis. Key Concepts Box 4-1 lists Guba's criteria for validity of qualitative research.

Maxwell's Criteria for Validity of Qualitative Research

More recently, Maxwell (1992) has adopted a stance more consistent with that of Wolcott (1990) that is, "that **understanding** is a more fundamental concept for qualitative research than validity" (p. 281). Maxwell's typology based on understanding includes *descriptive validity, interpretive validity, theoretical validity, generalizability,* and *evaluative validity.*

KEY CONCEPTS BOX 4-1

Guba's Criteria for Validity of Qualitative Research		
CRITERIA	**DEFINITION**	**STRATEGIES**
Credibility	The researcher's ability to take into account all of the complexities that present themselves in a study and to deal with patterns that are not easily explained.	Do prolonged participation at study site. Do persistent observation. Do peer debriefing. Practice triangulation. Collect "slice-of-life" data items. Do member checks. Establish structural corroboration or coherence. Establish referential adequacy.
Transferability	The researcher's belief that everything is context-bound.	Collect detailed descriptive data. Develop detailed descriptions of the context.
Dependability	The stability of the data.	Overlap methods. Establish an "audit trail."
Confirmability	The neutrality or objectivity of the data collected.	Practice triangulation. Practice reflexivity.

Descriptive Validity

Maxwell proposes that **descriptive validity,** or factual accuracy, is fundamental to any qualitative, descriptive account:

> The first concern of most qualitative researchers is with the factual accuracy of their account—that is, that they are not making up or distorting things they saw and heard. If you report that an informant made a particular statement in an interview, is this correct? (pp. 285–286).

According to this criteria, any matters related to descriptive validity could be validated by checking with the informant, or the tape-recorded or videotaped account of the interview that the quote that has been reproduced in the account is correct.

For example, in a study I was working on related to documenting the implementation of the National Council of Teachers of Mathematics (NCTM) Standards, I conducted interviews with teachers, principals, students, and the superintendents of districts throughout the United States and Canada. At one of these sites, the superintendent responded to a question about how best to change the way high school teachers teach math in the following way: "I think that the only way to change the way high school math teachers teach math is to line them up and shoot them!" In a case study I wrote about the site, I used the quote to illustrate the frustration the superintendent felt toward the implementation of the NCTM Standards in high schools in the district. When the account was shared with the participants in the study to check the accuracy of the story, the superintendent had a violent reaction to the quote. He responded to me that he never said such a thing and that the account bordered on "tabloid journalism."

To check the descriptive validity of the account, I returned to the taped interview, the transcript of the interview, and to my fieldnotes and the fieldnotes of my co-researcher who was present at the interview. Sure enough, the quote was accurate, and I felt justified in incorporating it into the account. The project director, however, was more concerned about the "potential harm" of the quote, and in a subsequent draft of the case study the account was "paraphrased." Nevertheless, I had established the descriptive validity of a questionable section of the account by returning to data sources to double-check the accuracy of what was said by whom.

Interpretive Validity

Maxwell describes **interpretive validity** as the concern researchers have with the meaning attributed to behaviors by the people who have been studied. That is, it is concern for what is commonly called the "participants' perspective":

> Interpretive accounts are grounded in the language of the people studied and rely as much as possible on their own words and concepts. The issue, again, is not the appropriateness of these concepts for the account, but their accuracy as applied to the perspective of the individuals included in the account. (Maxwell, 1992, p. 289)

To return to the story of the superintendent who was upset with my use of the "shoot the math teachers" quote, the issue was also related to interpretive validity.

How might someone at the site reading the account interpret the language of "line them up and shoot them"? For example, a high school math teacher in the district might interpret the remark as an indication that all high school math teachers in the district will be fired—literally! Indeed, this was not the superintendent's intent and on that basis alone was a good enough reason to change the account and forego the use of the quote.

Theoretical Validity

Theoretical validity refers to the ability of the research report to explain the phenomenon that has been studied and described:

> Theoretical validity thus refers to an account's validity as a *theory* of some phenomenon. Any theory has two components: the concepts or categories that the theory employs, and the relationships that are thought to exist among the concepts. (Maxwell, 1992, p. 291)

For example, to return to my superintendent's story, the language used by the superintendent to describe the difficult nature of changing high school math teaching might be labeled as an act that perpetuates the traditional power relationships that exist in school districts and the intractability of educational reform efforts in general. In order for this interpretation to be theoretically valid, the reader of the account would need to apply a theoretical construct to the description, and based on that theory, extrapolate to other aspects of the school community.

Generalizability

According to Maxwell, there are two aspects of **generalizability:** generalizability within the community that has been studied (internal generalizability) and generalizability to settings that were not studied by the researcher (external generalizability). Internal generalizability is more important than external generalizability because qualitative researchers (and action researchers) rarely make claims about the external generalizability of their research (Maxwell, 1992).

For example, my reliance on the data I had collected through an interview with the superintendent may have had descriptive and interpretive validity, but I may have missed other aspects of the superintendent's perspective that were not evident during the interview. In this case the internal generalizability of the account was threatened by the interpretation of the interview. However, by inviting the superintendent to respond to the account, I was able to add to the superintendent's perspective in his own words and to increase the internal generalizability of the account.

We will discuss the relevance of generalizability in greater detail later in this chapter.

Evaluative Validity

Evaluative validity has to do with whether the researcher was objective enough to report the data in as unbiased a way as possible instead of making judgments and evaluations of the data. No account is immune to questions of whether the teacher researcher was focusing on being evaluative instead of being concerned

Maxwell's Criteria for Validity of Qualitative Research	
CRITERIA	**DEFINITION**
Descriptive validity	Factual accuracy.
Interpretive validity	Concern for the participants' perspective.
Theoretical validity	The ability of the research report to explain the phenomenon that has been studied and described.
Generalizability	*Internal generalizability:* Generalizability within the community that has been studied. *External generalizability:* Generalizability to settings that were not studied by the researcher.
Evaluative validity	Whether the researcher was able to present the data without being evaluative or judgmental.

with describing and understanding the phenomenon that was studied. Clearly, the superintendent thought that I had "made up" the "shoot them" quote to make an evaluative statement about the superintendent and the district. I, on the other hand, maintained that my purpose in doing the research was to increase our understanding of the phenomenon under investigation—not to evaluate the mathematics programs in the district. Key Concepts Box 4–2 shows Maxwell's criteria for validity of qualitative research.

Anderson, Herr, and Nihlen's Criteria for Validity in Action Research

For most qualitative researchers, it is helpful to apply words such as *trustworthiness* and *understanding* to indicate the validity of our research. Using these criteria provides us with an opportunity (and challenge) to ensure that our research satisfies professional standards. However, Anderson et al. (1994) have argued that action researchers need a system for judging the quality of their inquiries that is specifically tailored to their classroom-based research projects:

> If practitioner researchers are to be accepted in a larger dialogue about education, they must develop some inquiry criteria for their research. This is not to say that they need to justify themselves by the same inquiry criteria as academic research, but rather that they must make the case for a different conception of validity. This conception of validity should respond to the purposes and conditions of practitioner research and the uniqueness of its contribution to the dialogue. (1994, p. 29)

To this end, Anderson et al. offer the following criteria for the validity of action research: *democratic validity, outcome validity, process validity, catalytic validity,* and *dialogic validity.*

Democratic Validity

Democratic validity requires that the multiple perspectives of all of the participants in the study (teachers, principals, parents, and students) have been accurately represented. The question for teacher researchers will be how to ensure that participants' multiple perspectives are captured. One way to ensure that there is democratic validity to an action research study will be to involve teachers and administrators in a collaborative effort with participants representing the group being studied. Make sure "the problems emerge from a particular context and solutions are appropriate to that context" (Cunningham, 1983, p. 30).

Outcome Validity

Outcome validity requires that the action emerging from a particular study leads to the successful resolution of the problem that was being studied. That is, your study can be considered valid if you learn something that can be applied to the subsequent research cycle. For example, James Reston's study of Eastview's absenteeism policy (see chapter 6) leads to a number of "findings" that affected the development of a new policy. These findings included a need to address

- The "respectfulness of students."
- Issues related to "feeling safe" in a school.
- The reteaching of conflict management skills.
- The feeling of children in the upper grades that school rules were unfair.
- Student perception that absenteeism added to the image of being "bad."
- The fact that 75% of the general school population and students with excessive absenteeism have attended the school for more than two years.

All of these outcomes led to action that has helped to address the school's absenteeism problems.

Process Validity

Process validity requires that a study has been conducted in a "dependable" and "competent" manner. It is possible in any study to find support for any feasible perspective. However, we engage in research processes that help us combat the tendency to present our studies as only glowing validations of existing exemplary practices! One way to address this issue is to be vigilant in reflecting on the suitability of your data collection techniques and to modify your strategies if the data you are collecting are not answering your questions.

Catalytic Validity

The criteria of **catalytic validity** require that the participants in a study are moved to take action on the basis of their heightened understanding of the subject of the study. The results of your study should serve as a "catalyst" for action! According to this schema, your action research effort is valid if it moves you and others involved to action (see chapter 6 on Action Planning).

Dialogic Validity

Dialogic comes from the word *dialogue*, to have a conversation. Thus, **dialogic validity** involves having a critical conversation with others about your research

Anderson's Criteria for Validity of Action Research	
CRITERIA	**TEST QUESTION**
Democratic validity	Have the multiple perspectives of all of the individuals in the study been accurately represented?
Outcome validity	Did the action emerging from the study lead to the successful resolution of the problem?
Process validity	Was the study conducted in a dependable and competent manner?
Catalytic validity	Were the results of the study a catalyst for action?
Dialogic validity	Was the study reviewed by peers?

findings and practices. Dialogic validity requires that the "goodness" of the research is established by application of a peer review process (similar to what already exists in traditional publication circles). For example, the teacher researchers with whom I work use an electronic bulletin board as a venue to share their research with the wider (cyberspace) professional community.

See Key Concepts Box 4–3 for Anderson's criteria for validity of action research.

Wolcott's Strategies for Ensuring the Validity of Action Research

Given this book's focus on qualitatively oriented action research, teacher researchers should pay close attention to the following strategies. Taken in concert with the previous discussion about validity criteria, they provide qualitatively oriented teacher researchers with practical options for making sure their research is the best it can be (adapted from Wolcott, 1994).

Talk Little, Listen a Lot

This strategy suggests that teacher researchers conducting interviews, asking questions, or engaging children, parents, and colleagues in discussions about the problem being studied ought to carefully monitor the ratio of listening to talking. For example, interviewing children can be difficult work—our best thought-out questions elicit painfully brief replies—and we are left wondering what to do next. As teachers we are in the business of talking for a living, so it comes quite naturally to us to jump in with our own answer for the child. The trustworthiness of our inquiries will be enhanced if we can bite our tongues, think of some other probing questions, and wait patiently (one thousand . . . two thousand . . . three thousand. . . !). As a teacher I have never been very comfortable with silence in my classroom, particularly when I thought that I had asked an engaging question. My advice is to be patient and allow the respondents time to respond. Avoid being your own best informant.

Record Observations Accurately

In conducting classroom research it is near impossible to record observations while you are teaching. It is important, however, that you record observations as soon as possible following a teaching episode to accurately capture the essence of what transpired. While audio and video recordings can assist with our efforts to record accurately, there will still be many occasions when, as participant observers, we have to rely on our fieldnotes, our journals, or our memories. And for me, relying on my memory is becoming an increasingly scary thing!

Begin Writing Early

In a work day already crunched by the pressures of time, finding time to write in journals is often problematic. However, if we rely solely on our memories of what has been happening in our classrooms over an extended period of time, we are likely to fall victim to writing romanticized versions of classroom and school life. Make time to write down your reflections. The act of writing down your recollections of a teaching episode, or observation will make evident to you what blanks need to be filled in, for example, what questions need to be asked the next day or what should be the focus of your observations.

Let Readers "See" for Themselves

Let readers "see" for themselves. That is, include primary data in any account to let the readers of your action research accounts (colleagues, principals, university professors) see the data for themselves. As Wolcott (1994) suggests, "In striking the delicate balance between providing too much detail and too little, I would rather err on the side of too much; conversely, between overanalyzing and underanalyzing data, I would rather say too little" (p. 350). This is particularly true in a school-wide action research effort in which you are seeking support for possible change on the basis of the provocative and persuasive data that is presented to teaching colleagues who may not have had a central role in the conduct of the study. When sharing your research reports with colleagues, let them see the data. This may mean using charts, graphs, photographs, film—whatever you have collected. But in so doing you will bring the recipient of your work along in the process and perhaps earn their buy-in to the next action research cycle. *Showing* can be more persuasive than telling.

Report Fully

In our quest to find neat answers and solutions to our problems, it is often easy to avoid keeping track of discrepant events and data. Just when we think we know the answer, some pieces of data come along to shatter the illusion of having neatly resolved the problem! We do not need to be fearful of discrepant data. After all, it is all grist for the research mill, and while we do not need to report everything, it is helpful to keep track of the discrepant data and to seek further explanation to understand what is happening in our classrooms/schools.

Be Candid

Teacher researchers should be candid about their work, and if writing a narrative that they hope to publish or share with a broader audience, they should make explicit any biases that they may have about the inquiry they have undertaken. Teacher researchers should also make explicit the things about which they have made judgments for it is easy to slip into a narrative that seeks to validate one's position. Being candid may also provide an opportunity to be explicit about events that occurred during the study and that may have affected the outcomes. For example, high student turnover rates may provide an explanation for fluctuating test scores.

Seek Feedback

It is always a good idea to seek feedback from colleagues (and perhaps even students, parents, volunteers, administrators) on your written study. Other readers will help raise questions about what you as the writer will have taken for granted. They will raise questions about the accuracy of the account and help us to go back to our classrooms in our quest to get the story right (or at least, not all wrong).

Write Accurately

Having written a description of your action research, it is a good idea for teacher researchers to read the account aloud or solicit the assistance of a close colleague in a careful reading of the account to look for contradictions in the text. We are often too close to the investigation to really see the contradictions in a story that may be blatantly obvious to an outsider. Although we are assuming in this discussion that teacher researchers will generate a written account of their action research efforts, we will see in chapter 7 some alternative formats that can be used for sharing the outcomes of an action research effort. Nevertheless, the accuracy of the account (whether written or "performed") is critical to the validity of the study. (For further discussion of these points and a discussion of "When It Really Matters, Does Validity Really Matter?" see Wolcott, 1994, pp. 348–370.) See Research in Action Checklist 4–1 for Wolcott's strategies for ensuring the validity of qualitative action research.

RESEARCH IN ACTION CHECKLIST 4–1

Wolcott's Strategies for Ensuring the Validity of Action Research
_____ Talk little; listen a lot.
_____ Record accurately.
_____ Begin writing early.
_____ Let readers "see" for themselves.
_____ Report fully.
_____ Be candid.
_____ Seek feedback.
_____ Write accurately.

Reliability

For our purposes, we will define **reliability** as the consistency that our data measures what we are attempting to measure over time. If we are using a particular instrument or test, we hope that it will give us the same results over time. If you have ever administered standardized tests to students, you will be familiar with the reliability coefficients that are presented in the administration manuals. The numbers are meant to convey to the test user the peace of mind that, if the test were administered on a future occasion, individual students would score roughly the same.

For qualitatively oriented action researchers the message here is simple—as you think about the results of your inquiry, consider whether you think that your data would be consistently collected if the same techniques were utilized over time. Or if you are working as a member of a team collecting data, work out how to resolve any differences among observers so you can agree on the descriptive accuracy of an account.

The Difference Between Reliability and Validity

To review, reliability "refers to the repeatability . . . of scientific observations" (Pelto & Pelto, 1978, p. 33). And as the following quotation suggests, reliability is closely related to validity:

> Reliability, in my view, refers not to an aspect of validity or to a separate issue from validity, but to a particular threat to validity. If different observers or methods produce descriptively different data or accounts of the same events or situations, this puts into question the descriptive validity (and other types of validity as well) of the accounts. (Maxwell, 1992, p. 288)

Reliability, however, is not the same thing as validity. Remember, a valid test that measures what it purports to measure will do so consistently over time. A reliable test may consistently measure the wrong thing!

Generalizability

Historically, research in education concerned itself with **generalizability**, a term that refers to the applicability of findings to settings and contexts different from the one in which they were obtained. That is, based on the behavior of a small group of individuals, researchers try to explain the behavior of a wider group of people. This view of generalizability, however, is not directly applicable to teacher action research—even though there is still a mindset among some teachers, administrators, and policy makers that the findings of action research studies should be transferable. Many of these people believe that we should be able to generalize from the outcomes of a study in one classroom, one school, and one district to all similar classrooms in the state or country. This is not the nature of the research we are engaged in.

The goal of action research is to understand what is happening in *your* school or classroom and to determine what might improve things in that context (Sagor, 1992). Therefore, action researchers don't need to worry about the generalizability of data because they are not seeking to define ultimate truths. However, one of the reviewers for this book had the following reaction to this dismissal of generalizability:

> I fear, however, that this approach lends credence to many of my colleagues' beliefs that action research is unscientific, biased, and not generalizable. Some go so far to call it "garbage research." The question that they often pose is what good is research that is not generalizable? (Anonymous reviewer)

Indeed, action research has faced a self-esteem problem among many "academics" who question the worthiness of the activity as "scientific" inquiry. Confronted with a similar argument, Stringer (1996) offered the following response:

> Whether or not action research is accepted as "scientific" depends on the way in which science is defined. Certainly it is, in one sense, rigorously empirical, insofar as it requires people to define clearly and observe the phenomenon under investigation. What is also evident, however, is that action research does not follow the carefully prescribed procedures that have become inscribed as scientific method. (p. 145)

Stringer goes on to argue that in spite of the success of the scientific method in advancing our knowledge in the "hard sciences," the applicability of this method to inquiries of human behavior has met with little success in increasing the predictability of human behavior. Other textbooks on educational research agree that action research is a different type of inquiry entirely and as such should not be focused on generalizability. For example, Vockell and Asher (1996) state:

> Action research refers to the practical application of the scientific method or other forms of disciplined inquiry to the process of dealing with everyday problems. It is particularly focused on teachers and other educators doing action research in order to make their particular educational activities more productive. It is more concerned with specific classes and programs and less concerned with generalized conclusions about other classes and programs. (p. 10)

Action research is *not* "garbage research" at the classroom/school level. As teacher researchers we are challenging the experimental researcher's view that the only credible research is that which can be generalized to a larger population. Many examples of teacher research are generalizable to other classroom settings, but the power of action research is not in its generalizability. It is in the *relevance* of the findings to the researcher or the audience of the research.

Personal Bias in the Conduct of Action Research

Related to the issue of generalizability of research is the issue of personal bias. If we conduct our research in a systematic, disciplined manner, we will go a long way toward minimizing personal bias in our findings. However, in an intimate activity such as action research, it is a challenge to remain "objective" and open, to look into the mirror of our findings and reflect on what we see. It is relatively easy in any research, should we choose to, to collect data that simply validates our existing practices, to maintain the status quo, to pat ourselves on the collective back, and to ignore discrepant data or discredit research results. The same can be said for reviewing related literature—we may choose to review only the literature that supports a particular thesis we wish to promote. None of these are acceptable approaches for reconciling the biased collection of data.

Propositions

One way for teacher researchers to get in touch with their biases about the subject they are investigating is to develop a list of propositions about what they think they will find during the course of their investigations. These propositions provide a window into the belief system and personal biases that can, and often do, creep into the investigation. These statements also provide a good starting point for examining teacher researchers' theories about teaching and learning and where they came from.

For example, a teacher who wishes to investigate the effects of manipulatives on student achievement in mathematics may generate propositions such as:

1. The use of manipulatives when teaching mathematics will increase students' conceptual knowledge of mathematics.
2. The use of manipulatives will help overcome math anxiety because the children will have more fun doing math.
3. The use of manipulatives will improve students' basic number facts skills.

A closer examination of these propositions is a useful activity for exploring what the teacher researchers believe they will find before they start their investigations and what they might do to ensure that they remain vigilant in the fidelity with which they collect their data (thus addressing the concerns of researcher bias). Similarly, this activity helps to clarify teacher researchers' conceptual frameworks for their investigations by making explicit the theories that affect what they do before, during, and after the research.

Doing the Right Thing: The Role of Ethics in Action Research

Simply stated, the role of ethics in action research can be considered in terms of how each of us treats the individuals with whom we interact at our school setting: students, parents, volunteers, administrators, and teaching colleagues. "At a commonsense level, caring, fairness, openness, and truth seem to be the important values undergirding the relationships and the activity of inquiring" (Smith, 1990, p. 260). However, values such as these invariably take on a different meaning for different people with whom we interact. Nevertheless, it is critical to the success of your action research project that there is a clear understanding of the intimate nature of the research process and that participants are not "wronged" in the name of research.

The vignette of Billabong Elementary School that opened this chapter is a good reminder of why it is important to think about ethical dilemmas **before** they occur. And while I have seen few instances of where ethical dilemmas have threatened to stall a collaborative action research effort, the very nature of the enterprise provides the potential for conflict and harm. Considering the ethics of action research before commencing the work is one way to ensure that you are prepared to respond in an ethical, caring manner to difficult situations that may arise.

The issue of ethics in qualitative research and action-oriented research has received considerable attention in recent years (c.f., Smith, 1990, Soltis, 1990, Wolcott, 1990, Eisner, 1991, and Flinders, 1992). Most of this literature describes mistakes made in the research process and how the ethics of the situation were addressed. What makes the subject of ethics particularly challenging for teacher researchers is the intimate and open-ended nature of action research.

Action research is intimate because there is little distance between teacher researchers and their subjects—the students in their classrooms and schools. Qualitatively oriented action research is open ended because the direction of the research often unfolds during the course of the study. This significantly complicates the ability of teacher researchers to obtain participants' "fully informed consent" to participate in the research process. **Informed consent** is central to research ethics. It is the principle that seeks to ensure that all human subjects retain autonomy and the ability to judge for themselves what risks are worth taking for the purpose of furthering scientific knowledge.

In action research the key participants in a study are often the students in our classrooms. How does the concept of informed consent apply to them? Do we need to obtain written permission from parents/guardians before collecting naturally occurring data such as test scores, observations, work samples, and so on? Probably not. But as you will see in the following discussion, it is important that you develop your own criteria for what is considered to be *ethical* behavior.

Ethical Guideposts

The following commonsense ethical guideposts may help teacher researchers respond appropriately when faced with ethical decisions before, during, and after an action research inquiry (adapted from Smith, 1990).

Ethical Perspective

Researchers Should Have an Ethical Perspective That Is Very Close to Their Personal Ethical Position. This may seem like a statement of the obvious except for the caveat that as teacher researchers we may find ourselves in situations that are foreign to us. For example, in a collaborative action research project focused on the effects of a new math problem-solving curriculum on student achievement and attitude, teachers are asked to administer a student attitude survey. The surveys are then analyzed by a team of teacher researchers representing different grades or benchmark levels in the school. During the analysis, it becomes clear that one group of students is very unhappy with their math instruction and have supported their assertions with negative comments about the teacher. What will you do with the data? Should they be shared in an unedited form with the teacher? Who stands to be hurt in the process? What potential good can come from sharing the data? Or, perhaps the principal hears that there is a problem with one teacher and asks for access to the data so that the teacher can be placed on a "plan of assistance." How should the research team respond? What assurances of confidentiality were given to the participants prior to collecting the data? How will you respond to the principal when stopped in the hallway and asked for your opinion?

This scenario is not meant to scare you away from doing action research. However, these are the unexpected outcomes that occasionally face teacher researchers who have been made privy to information about their own teaching and that of their colleagues. Smith's lesson is an important one. You will potentially avoid such awkward situations if you have clarified your own ethical perspectives at the outset. This might take the form of a values clarification activity that can be undertaken individually or collectively. The point is this—be prepared to respond in a manner that is comfortable and natural for you. When you are placed in the "hot seat," there may not be time to give a well thought out, rational response. This situation will be easier if you can respond in a personal manner.

Informed Consent

Informed Consent Should Take the Form of a Dialogue That Mutually Shapes the Research and the Results. Be clear about whether you need to seek permission from participants in the study. This may be determined by discussing the action research project with an administrator or central office person who can describe instances that necessitate written permission. For example, if you are using photographs or videotapes as data collection techniques and intend to use these artifacts in a public forum, such as presentation at a conference, make sure that you have checked whether written permission is necessary. The answer may vary from district to district depending on how the materials are to be used.

Similarly, consider how to inform students that they are subjects in a study. For example, you may decide to interview a small group to determine how a problem-solving curriculum is being implemented in different classrooms as a follow up to a survey or an observation. How will you ensure the anonymity of the respondents to protect their privacy? How will you protect the confidentiality of participants? Confidentiality is important for the following reasons:

- Confidentiality is intended to protect research informants from stress, embarrassment, or unwanted publicity.
- Confidentiality protects participants in situations where the information they reveal to a researcher can be used against them by others. (Flinders, 1992)

Confidentiality usually involves the use of pseudonyms to conceal identities. However, protecting confidentiality in a qualitatively oriented action-research effort is sometimes more problematic than just assigning pseudonyms. For example, a team of teacher researchers responsible for driving a schoolwide action research effort will likely be made privy to the intimate details of their colleagues' classrooms. It will be their challenge to make sure that they protect their colleagues from stress, embarrassment, or unwanted publicity that may come from sharing the action research findings. And of course, all of this must be balanced against their commitment to improve the learning experiences of the students in their school.

Social Principles

You should be able to identify broader social principles that are an integral part of who you are as a teacher and a contributing member of the community in which you live. These broader social principles should dictate your ethical stance. For example, democratic processes, social justice, equality, and emancipation may be the principles that guide your ethical behavior in a given situation.

Flinders' Conceptual Framework for Ethics in Qualitative Research

Flinders' (1992) offers a useful conceptual framework for guiding ethical conduct in qualitative research, a framework that is worth consideration by teacher researchers. Flinders provides the following conceptual framework: *utilitarian*, *deontological*, *relational*, and *ecological ethics*. In your efforts to clarify values, it may be worthwhile to consider the issues raised by these four perspectives and how resolving these issues can contribute to your personal/professional ethical stance.

Utilitarian Ethics

The central tenet of **utilitarian ethics** is the notion of the greatest good for the greatest number or whether more good than harm is likely to be produced by a given decision. This principle of utility can be applied by teacher researchers who must struggle with whether the findings of their study have the potential to significantly improve the experiences of children while conforming to the concepts of informed consent, confidentiality, and avoidance of harm. We have already discussed informed consent and confidentiality, but this last concept can be a challenge to rationalize.

Avoidance of harm morally bounds teacher researchers to conduct their inquiries in a manner that minimizes potential harm to those involved in the study—students, teachers, parents, administrators, and volunteers. This concept is obvious in the medical profession where participants' physical well-being may be placed at risk by virtue of being a subject in an experimental study and receiving a radical treatment (for example, a new HIV/AIDS vaccine). This concept, however, is less obvious in an educational setting. A broader view of this concept suggests that teacher researchers need to convey with confidence to action research participants that they will not suffer harm as the result of their involvement in the research effort.

Teacher researchers must remain sensitive to their colleagues' fears of participating in an action research effort and remain vigilant in their efforts to protect participants from harm. Similarly, it is important to assure parents that their children are not being used as laboratory rats in some poorly conceived clinical experiment that could potentially harm them. As teachers, we typically do not administer "treatments" or "experimental interventions" to children. However, as a result of focusing on a particular problem and immersing ourselves in the relevant literature, we may design an instructional or curriculum intervention to address a perceived need.

Deontological Ethics

Simply stated, **deontological ethics** can be seen as the ethics of "duty and obligation." From this perspective an action may bring about good results, but it is not deontologically correct unless that action also conforms to ethical standards such as honesty and justice. From this perspective, acting ethically may be viewed in terms of "doing unto others as you would have them do unto you!" For example, it would clearly be unethical to deceive participants in an action research study or to simply treat them as research pawns—a means to an end.

As you begin to clarify your personal, ethical perspective it is worthwhile to reflect on how you would want to be treated as a participant in a research study. How would you feel if you were deceived by the researchers? What action would you take? How can you prevent research participants from feeling exploited? Again, there are no simple answers to these ethical questions.

Relational Ethics

Flinders writes that "a proponent of **relational ethics** would readily accept that moral behavior often upholds utilitarian standards by leading to good consequences for individuals, communities, or society at large" (1992, p. 106). From this perspective, collaboration in an action research effort would necessitate that the team members work out mutually beneficial agreements for everyone who participates in the inquiry. This would include working, talking, and debating together to help each person achieve individual and collective goals. The members of an action research team, however, do not have to unconditionally accept an individual participant's teaching performance as "best practice." From this perspective, you may be may be faced with making a nonjudgmental assessment of colleagues' teaching and the possibility that friends and colleagues do not agree with the portrayal and interpretation of test results, surveys, interviews, and observation data, for example.

Ecological Ethics

Proponents of **ecological ethics** are culturally sensitive to the taken-for-granted aspects of our social and professional lives. From this perspective, the teacher researcher must remain attentive to the relationships between the researcher and the participants—a relationship that is determined by "roles, status, language, and cultural norms" (Flinders, 1992, p. 108). The lesson for teacher researchers who are proponents of this perspective is to pay attention to the research processes of

Ethical Guideposts for Teacher Researchers

_____ Develop an ethical perspective that is close to your personal, ethical position.
_____ Seek your action research participants' informed consent.
_____ Determine the broader social principles that affect your ethical stance.
_____ Consider the principles of utilitarian, deontological, relational, and ecological ethics in developing your ethical position.
_____ Consider confidentiality and anonymity and avoid harm.

giving information, reciprocity, and collaboration and to be sensitive to how these processes are viewed by other participants in the action research cycle. Again, this perspective forces us to confront the socially responsive characteristics of our research efforts as being democratic, equitable, liberating, and life enhancing.

The purpose of this discussion on ethics in action research has been to prepare you to think about a whole range of issues that face any researcher. Carefully consider how you will respond when confronted with difficult questions from colleagues, parents, students, and administrators. Taking time to clarify your values and ethical perspectives will help you respond in a professional, personal, and caring fashion.

As you embark on your action research journey and data collection efforts, remember that you are ultimately condemned to freedom in matters of ethics (Eisner, 1991, p. 226). There are few absolutes. Working with colleagues through issues related to confidentiality, anonymity, informed consent, and rational judgment in matters of ethics will ensure that you avoid potentially difficult situations that may arise in implementing your action research effort. (See Research in Action Checklist 4–2 for ethical guideposts for teacher researchers.)

Summary

This chapter has examined validity, reliability, and generalizability and how they affect the conduct of action research. **Validity** is a test of whether the data we collect accurately gauge what we are trying to measure. Reviewing the criteria for validity proposed by Guba, Maxwell, Anderson et al., and Wolcott will help ensure valid action research is the outcome of the data collection phase of the action research process.

Reliability is a measure of the consistency with which our data measure what we are attempting to measure over time. **Generalizability** refers to the applicability of research findings to settings and contexts different from the one in which they were obtained. In its strictest sense, however, generalizability is not directly applicable to teacher action research because of its highly contextualized nature.

Teacher researchers should recognize their own personal biases as much as possible and develop an ethical perspective that ensures they will do the right thing when confronted with a difficult ethical dilemma.

For Further Thought

1. How have you addressed the issues of validity, reliability, and generalizability in your action research inquiry?

2. Revisit the Billabong Elementary School vignette at the beginning of this chapter. Consider the questions that faced the action research team including:

   a. What do we do with the data that provided a negative picture of individual teachers in the school? Do we share data on an individual basis with teachers who were singled out by students? What risks do we run in sharing this information? How can we promote professional development without hurting anyone?

   b. What do we do with the data that indicated a great deal of dissatisfaction with how the principal had mandated the choice of curriculum? Do we risk alienating the teachers from the administration? Could some teachers be hurt professionally by action the principal might take?

   c. How can we improve student achievement through the use of technology without hurting teachers (and the principal) in the process?

   Be prepared to justify and defend your ethical positions in light of the ethical guideposts (ethical perspective, informed consent, social principles) and conceptual frameworks (utilitarian, deontological, relational, and ecological) presented in this chapter.

3. How would you characterize your ethical stance? What is your ethical perspective, your approach to informed consent, and your sense of the broader social principles that dictate your actions?

CHAPTER 5

Data Analysis
and Interpretation

After collecting your data, the next steps in the action research process are to review what you have learned and draw conclusions about what you think your data mean. This chapter provides guidelines and techniques for data analysis (the attempt to fully and accurately summarize and represent the data that has been collected) and data interpretation (the attempt to find meaning in that data, to answer the question "So what?").

This chapter provides a simple overview of descriptive statistics. Measures of central tendency (mean, mode, and median) and a measure of variability (standard deviation) are presented as appropriate data analysis techniques for teacher researchers who have collected measurable data.

———

After reading this chapter you should be able to

1. Define data analysis and data interpretation.
2. Identify appropriate data analysis techniques for your action research project.
3. Identify appropriate data interpretation techniques for your action research project.
4. Apply descriptive statistics, when appropriate, to the analysis of your data.

Emphasizing Learning by Deemphasizing Grades

LAUREN FAGEL, PAUL SWANSON, JOHN GORLESKI, AND JOE SENESE, HIGHLAND PARK HIGH SCHOOL

Lauren Fagel, Paul Swanson, John Gorleski, and Joe Senese are all members of the Action Research Laboratory (ARL) at Highland Park High School (HPHS) near Chicago, Illinois. This project provides a good example of a team approach to collaborative action research and the kinds of analysis and interpretations that can flow from various data sources.

The scene is a common one for teachers: Papers are returned to students who immediately search for the grade, sigh, take out calculators, tabulate quarter grades, and then compare grades with their neighbors! The rich comments and constructive feedback on the papers usually go unheeded—the all-important grade takes the prime focus of the students' gazes!

This study was conducted at Highland Park High School, one of two large public high schools in Township District 113. Our student population consists of 1509 students with an ethnic makeup of 3% Asian, 2% African American, 13% Hispanic, and 82% White. Ninety-two percent of the student body is college-bound, and the parent community strongly encourages high student achievement. Many students enroll in Advanced Placement (AP) classes, strive to become members of the Highland Park Honor Society, and compete to become senior class valedictorian or salutatorian. This ARL group, which was made up of an English teacher, a health teacher, and a history teacher, was concerned about the immense amount of pressure put on students to receive good grades. We questioned the number system teachers use to assign grades, and we wondered whether grades actually represent what students learn. We discussed the role of the teacher as assessor, questioning whether we act as true evaluators of student work or simply as "sorters" of students. We lamented the all-encompassing role grades play in the HPHS academic environment. We decided to conduct research in this area, investigating how a deemphasis of grades could, in turn, emphasize learning in the classroom. The research questions were as follows:

1. How does an elimination of number and letter grades throughout the year (with the exception of quarter and semester grades) affect student attitudes toward learning?

2. How does an elimination of number and letter grades throughout the year (with the exception of quarter and semester grades) affect our teaching styles, use of assessments, and choice of curriculum materials?

3. How does an extensive use of student self-assessment affect student growth, improvement, and achievement over the course of a school year?

4. How does deemphasizing grades allow us to enrich our teaching?

We began the year by informing students of our involvement in the ARL and presenting a rationale for deemphasizing grades and emphasizing learning. Teachers were still required to assign a grade at the end of each quarter, and students were curious about how their final grade would be determined. We explained how the system would work and followed up by asking students to write down what they thought they would like about the system, what they thought they would not like, and what they did not understand. A letter was also sent home to parents explaining the system and encouraging them to contact us with any questions, concerns, or comments.

Approximately once a month we met as a team for an entire day of reflection, discussion, brainstorming, and future planning. We quickly found out that certain aspects of our system were working, while others needed refining, and still others needed to be eliminated or replaced.

With the exception of one major project during third quarter, we returned all student work without a number or letter grade. Instead, we used several different types of markings to indicate to students how well they performed on a particular assessment. On homework assignments, including journal entries, we wrote comments and then assigned a $\checkmark$, $\checkmark+$, or $\checkmark-$. On long-term projects, we either assessed different aspects of the final product on a scale of 1 to 5 and wrote one or two sentences to the student, or we did not use any scale and instead wrote extensive comments. On tests and quizzes we marked objective items wrong when appropriate, assigned a $\sqrt{}$, $\sqrt{}+$, or $\sqrt{}-$ to short-answer and other types of subjective questions, and wrote general comments throughout the test or quiz. Most students were able to tell how well they performed on a particular assessment, and only a very few students persisted by asking us how our comments would translate into a letter grade. In these cases, we found that students were less argumentative than our students had been in the previous year (prior to deemphasizing grades). This year we found ourselves more open to criticism about the way test questions were written and exams formatted because students seemed to be more genuine in their questioning. They were not arguing for points because there were no points! This created a more community-like setting in the classroom, with all of us aiming for the same goal—learning.

Self-Assessment Worksheet

After some modification during the first semester, we adopted a self-assessment worksheet that encouraged students to reflect on their progress periodically throughout the year. The worksheet included the following headings: Content Mastery, Skill Mastery, Completion of Work, and In-Class Activity. This worksheet evolved into an end of quarter self-evaluation that asked students to select a grade they felt they deserved and then to provide evidence by referring to specific assignments, tests, quizzes, and projects. Finally, by the end of the school year, we were using an end-of-quarter evaluation sheet that listed the student's mid-quarter grade range, the marks they received on specific homework assignments completed since the previous student-teacher-parent conference, and a general comment for each major test, quiz, and project they had completed since mid-quarter. Students' grades were then assigned without holding an end-of-quarter conference.

Another important part of this project was that students accepted responsibility for their grades and participated in developing criteria that would be used to assess the quality of work. The following criteria are an example of what evolved from involving students in the decision-making process:

"A" Criteria

   Participates actively in class
   Shows a great deal of effort
   Does all homework
   Does well on tests
   Is on time for class
   Shows respect and works well with others
   Is always prepared

"B" Criteria

   Shows good participation
   Misses no more than 1 to 2 assignments
   Has 1 to 2 tardies
   Shows good knowledge of material
   Has no unauthorized absences
   Shows some effort
   Demonstrates respect for others

"C" Criteria

   Demonstrates some knowledge of material and passes all tests
   Work is frequently late or not turned in
   Rarely participates in class
   Shows little effort
   Has several tardies
   Has unauthorized absences
   Is frequently not prepared

"D" Criteria

   Doesn't show knowledge of material and performs poorly on tests
   Has large number of assignments not turned in
   Shows no effort or participation
   Shows little respect for others
   Has several unauthorized absences
   Is disruptive in class
   Is often tardy

By using this rubric, students had guidelines they could use as a reference to accurately assess their performance. The onus on defending a grade now became the students' responsibility and not the teachers'. If students could justify their self-evaluation grade, based on the criteria we had agreed to, that was the grade they received. As a result of this ownership, students had few complaints regarding their grades.

Student-Teacher Conferences

Students appeared to have a difficult time assigning and defending their grades during student-teacher conferences. For many years students had been conditioned to accept the grades given to them by a teacher without question. They had rarely been asked to participate actively in assigning their own grade. The most valuable part of these conferences was the opportunity to speak with all students and to get a sense of how they were feeling about the class in general. Often the discussion of grade came at the end of the conference and was the shortest part of the conversation. Students were asked to suggest a grade (before the teacher), but there was a sense that a guessing game was in progress as we tried to balance the teacher's expectations with those of individual students.

The data collected from surveys, observations, and interviews with children suggest that the majority of students were either happy with the grading system or neutral about it. A majority of students indicated that the alternative grading system did affect their academic preparation and performance in class (in a positive way), and that they had a more positive attitude toward the class.

Grades

As we reflected on grade distributions comparing this year to the previous year, there appeared to be a significant increase in the number of students whose grades fell in the A/A- range (55% this year compared to 27% last year). There is no way of knowing exactly what accounted for the increase of A's and A-'s; however, we believe that students' involvement in deciding their own grade, as well as the less objective nature of the way grades were assigned (that is, not entirely based on the percentages scored on tests), had something to do with the outcomes. We believe that the increased focus on personal learning, growth, and improvement that evolved from deemphasizing grades made it less likely for students to fail and more likely for students to accept responsibility for their learning and to provide the evidence that they had learned.

The end-of-year survey revealed that 71% of students agreed with the following statement: "I feel that the grading practices used in this course helped me to focus more on my learning than on my grade." Another 74% agreed that "they would recommend that this teacher continue using these grading practices because they help students learn better." We believe that these kinds of statements indicate student support for our deemphasized grading practices and that learning can occur in an environment where the pressure to earn grades is reduced. Students made supporting comments such as these:

"I felt I could concentrate on education."
"It helped me concentrate on improving myself."
"It helps you focus more on information and less on what the teacher wants."
"It relieved a lot of stress and I was able to work at my ability without the competition of grades."
"In comparison to the traditional grading system, this system is the most effective way of assessing my level of performance."
"This method helps me perform best because it's personal to my needs."

It was very reassuring to us to see the pride that students showed and the importance they placed on giving accurate self-evaluation grades. The following two comments illustrate the integrity with which the majority of students approached this responsibility:

"I knew I had to be honest with myself."
"Integrity defines you, and if you die tomorrow, people won't remember your grades or your statistics; they remember how true and real you were with yourself."

We learned a tremendous amount through this research, but like any research we were left with more questions than we answered. For example:

- Is the total elimination of letter and number grades (with the exception of quarter and semester grades) the best way to deemphasize grades?
- Is there a way to deemphasize grades that requires less paperwork on the teacher's part?

(After all, one of things we learned through the implementation of this intervention is that grades are expedient and convenient for a harried teacher!)

- What is an appropriate role for students to play in determining their own grades?
- How can we deemphasize grades and still maintain very specific criteria/outcomes for students?

By far the most rewarding part of working on an action research team was the opportunity to learn and grow with a small group of teacher colleagues. This experience of mutual commitment provided a wonderful staff development experience; by working with these colleagues consistently throughout the year, we were able to explore new ideas and take risks in the classroom with a type of "safety net" in place. For that reason alone, as well as our desire to explore the new questions and challenges raised by our research, we will continue to conduct action research into the effectiveness of our teaching and grading practices.

Giving up grading practices and beliefs that we have held for years can be a very scary proposition. It is not always easy to turn over some of our control to others. Perhaps our first action research steps need to be "baby steps." This action research project freed us from the grading merry-go-round and provided a new way to address assessment issues. By taking these steps we were able to devote less time to pencil pushing and calculator crunching and to spend more time with our most important job: helping our students reach their full potential as we strive to reach our full potential as teachers.

PERHAPS THE MOST difficult part of action research is the process of trying to make sense of the mountains of data collected over the course of the study. This task is often daunting for action researchers who, engaged in the regular, ongoing collection of data, must change their focus and adopt a more analytical and interpretive lens. They must move beyond the description of the phenomenon they have studied and to make sense of what they have learned.

The Highland Park High School example richly illustrates how a team of teachers worked together to increase their understanding of how deemphasizing grades could help reemphasize student learning. In so doing, the teachers were able to encapsulate the "findings" of their research into "sound bites" that could be shared with other teachers and participants.

Considering how to best proceed with data analysis and data interpretation is critical before, during, and after the action research process. That is, it is important to think about "How am I going to make sense of this data?" prior to conducting the study to avoid collecting data that is not important or data that comes in a form that cannot be understood. Similarly, during the study, teacher researchers should reflect on what they are finding and how it can inform their ongoing data collection efforts. Finally, as the systematic collection of data winds up, teacher researchers should determine what they want to celebrate in their findings.

Ongoing Analysis and Reflection

Action research studies provide teacher researchers with data that can be used formatively and summatively. That is, much of the qualitative data collected during the study can be used to positively affect teaching throughout the study. For example, teachers have always reflected on their teaching before, during, and after a particular teaching episode—it's part of our professional disposition. Action research is no different. We can and should take time to analyze our data during the study to decide if what we are learning is what we had hoped to learn. For example, the HPHS team discovered early in their research that some aspects of their deemphasized grading system were working while others needed to be refined or eliminated. Pausing to analyze and reflect during the action research process is essential.

Anderson et al. (1994) maintain that "it is very important to recognize that at various intervals you must stop gathering data and reflect on what you have thus far" (p. 155). For example, they suggest that teacher researchers answer two questions to guide their work and reflections:

1. Is your research question still answerable and worth answering?
2. Are your data collection techniques catching the kind of data you wanted and filtering out the data that you don't? (p. 155)

Consciously "pausing" during the investigation will allow you to reflect on what you are attending to and what you are leaving out. Such a reflective stance will continue to guide your efforts (in process) as well as to allow for early "hunches" about what you are seeing so far. As Anderson et al. suggest:

Stopping periodically in the data collection process also allows you to see if you have any gaps in the data, holes where you need data to answer the questions. Seeing this early on in the research allows you to develop the correct techniques for a complete study. (1994, p. 156)

Another way to think of this is in terms of Lewin's original action research model and the attention given to rethinking, reflecting, discussing, replanning, understanding, and learning during the action research process.

Avoid Premature Action

While ongoing analysis and reflection is a natural part of the action research process, it is important to avoid premature actions based on early analysis and interpretation of data. Action researchers—especially inexperienced ones—often make rash or impulsive decisions based on limited or no data. Neophyte teacher researchers engaged in the first systematic study of their own teaching tend to zealously collect, analyze, and interpret data in a rapid-fire fashion. Their efforts go awry as they become their own best informants and jump to hasty conclusions and impulsive actions.

The action research process takes time. Teacher researchers must be wary of the lure of quick-fix strategies and patient enough to avoid the pitfalls of basing actions on premature analysis. Rarely will a few days of observation provide you with enough insight to enact a quick-fix strategy! Although it is much easier to start a study with a preconceived notion about what you will find, it's a far greater test of patience, endurance, and integrity to let the action research inquiry slowly unfold over the course of a semester or two.

The Role of Analysis and Interpretation

You will reach a point in the research process at which you will want to summarize for your colleagues what you have learned and what you think it means for your students. You will want to share your findings without having to share all of your data and use these findings to identify what will happen next in the action research process. This critical component of the action research process is called data analysis and interpretation, and it needs to be carefully thought out.

Data analysis is an attempt by the teacher researcher to summarize the data that have been collected in a dependable, accurate, reliable, and correct manner. It is the presentation of the findings of the study in a manner that has an air of undeniability (Wolcott, 1994). Alternatively, data interpretation is an attempt by the researcher to find meaning in the data, to answer the question "So what?" In other words, data analysis tries to report the outcomes or findings of the data collected, and data interpretation focuses on the implications or meaning of those findings.

When analyzing and interpreting data, challenge yourself to explore every angle. We have to examine the information we have collected and try to find patterns and seek out new understandings. Remember Deborah South from the chapter 1 vignette on "How to motivate unmotivated students"? At first, she was convinced that the only feasible interpretation of her data was that her class and her teaching were the causes of the dramatic drop in students' scores. After all, it was the only experience these eighteen students had in common during the term! However, as Deborah revisited her data and her fellow action researchers pushed her to examine other possibilities, it became clear that the homogeneous grouping of "low-achieving" and "unmotivated" students contributed to a "critical mass of negativity" in the classroom. As a result of her commitment to quality data analysis and interpretation, Deborah was able to use her action research findings to make a persuasive argument for the school principal to investigate other "interventions" that might more effectively address the problems of the "unmotivated" student.

Data Analysis Techniques

Picture this: After weeks (months, years) of data collection using a variety of qualitative data collection techniques (observations, interviews, surveys, audiotapes, and the like), you sit in your living room (classroom, faculty lounge) with colleagues (or by yourself perhaps being observed by a curious significant other!) surrounded by files (boxes) of stuff (data in all shapes and forms)! This less-than-romantic image of the teacher researcher is a common one. Having immersed themselves in the systematic study of a significant problem, teachers (individually and collectively) are confronted with the somewhat daunting task of data analysis, engaging in analysis that will represent the mountains of descriptive data in a "correct," "accurate," "reliable," and "right" way. There is no easy way to do this work: it is difficult, time-consuming, and challenging. And yet, it is potentially the most important step in the action research process as we try to understand what we have learned through our investigations.

The techniques outlined in the following sections will serve as guideposts and prompts to move you through your analysis as efficiently as possible. There is no substitute for taking time to fully immerse yourself in your data. Literally bury yourself in what you have.

Read and reread, listen and relisten, watch and rewatch. Get to know intimately what you have collected. Struggle with the nuances and caveats, the subtleties, the persuasive, the incomplete. Avoid premature judgment and action and try to remain aware of what will ultimately improve the lives of the children in your care. These are lofty goals, but they are at the heart of what we are trying to achieve.

Identifying Themes

One place to start your analysis is to work inductively as you begin to analyze the data: Consider the big picture and start to list "themes" that you have seen emerge in your literature review and in the data collection. Are there patterns that emerge, such as events that keep repeating themselves, key phrases that participants use to describe their feelings, or survey responses that seem to "match" one another? Consider the Highland Park High School action research team. As they gathered their data, they realized that they were dealing with many recurrent themes in their efforts to deemphasize grades—the stress on students created by grades, the satisfaction gained from the renewed focus on learning, the amount of time it took for teachers to assess student work not using traditional grades, and the issues of honesty and integrity, for example.

Coding Surveys, Interviews, and Questionnaires

One of the most frequent data analysis activities undertaken by action researchers is **coding**, the process of trying to find patterns and meaning in data collected through the use of surveys, interviews, and questionnaires. Working with these types of data is common because surveys, interviews, and questionnaires are generally accepted as part of the school culture, and they provide a great deal of information in a relatively short amount of time.

As you analyze your data, you may need to reduce that data to a manageable form. One way to proceed when working with fieldnotes, transcripts of taped interviews, pictures, maps, charts and so on is to try to record data on 3 X 5 index cards that are manageable and allow for sorting. As you read and reread through your data (possibly now reduced to your cards), compile your data in categories or themes. While there is nothing magical about this process, it does take time and a willingness to check that the mountains of descriptive data have been analyzed in a "correct," "accurate," "reliable," and "right" way.

If you can imagine playing cards and not knowing what the symbols on the cards mean, the following analogy might work: You have a deck of cards with each card containing data. The order of the cards is random. As you initially scan the cards you have an intuitive sense that the data on some of the cards looks similar to other cards. You finish carefully looking at all of the cards and reshuffle the deck. Again you look through the deck, but this time you group together the cards (data) that look alike. You end up with thirteen collections of four cards that have some kind of trait in common (the number or face value of the card). Again, you reshuffle the cards. This time as you start to sort through the cards, you notice a different theme (the suit of the card) and end up with four piles of thirteen cards. Puzzling. Not to be thwarted in your efforts, you again reshuffle the deck and attempt to settle on an organizing theme. You group together cards (data) that have sufficient common characteristics that you feel confident that your analysis of the data is undeniably accurate. But there is just one problem: What do you do with the Joker that found its way into the pack?! And what about that wildcard?! Where did they come from and where do they fit?! Just when you thought you had it all worked out, in crept something that challenges the themes you have used to organize and represent the data you have collected. The shuffling and sorting continues.

A few common sense guidelines may make this somewhat overwhelming activity of coding mountains of data more manageable:

1. Read through all of the data and attach working labels to blocks of text. These labels ought to have meaning for you—a kind of shorthand that will serve as a reference point when you return to the text later in the process.
2. Literally cut and paste the blocks of text onto 3 × 5 cards (similar to the card-playing analogy earlier) so that you now have the data in a manageable form. Use some kind of numbering system so that you can track the block of text back to the original context in which it appeared. For example, date and time (1/26 10:15) helps us locate the reference in our journal or fieldnotes. Remember: Context is important and you will want to check that you have correctly labeled the text you are trying to funnel into a category with similar text. Trying to shuffle reams of paper can be a difficult task so cards are a preferable way to work.
3. Start to group together cards that have the same or similar labels on them.
4. Revisit each pile of cards and see if in fact the label still fits or whether similar labels actually warrant their own category. This process is not dissimilar to brainstorming and seeking categories that will encapsulate similar thoughts and ideas.

Asking Key Questions

Another approach to data analysis involves the use of key questions. According to Stringer, working through a series of questions can enable action researchers to "extend their understanding of the problems and contexts" (1996, p. 87) they have investigated. These key questions may be the very questions with which you began your action research inquiry, the questions mentioned in chapter 2 that involve the who, what, where, when, why, and how of the educational process. For example: Who is centrally involved? Who has resources? Which ones? What major activities, events, or issues are relevant to the problem? How do acts, activities, and events happen? When does this problem occur? and so on. While not all of these questions will be applicable to any single situation, they may provide a starting point for teacher researchers who are engaged individually or collectively in analysis.

To illustrate, the Highland Park High School team raised questions such as What is an appropriate role for students to play in determining their own grades? How can grades be deemphasized while teachers maintain very specific criteria/outcomes for students? Answers to these questions (and others) will help extend the team's understanding of the problems associated with deemphasizing grades while emphasizing the importance of learning.

Doing an Organizational Review

Another approach Stringer suggests is undertaking an organizational review that focuses on the following features of the organization (in this case, a school): vision and mission, goals and objectives, structure of the organization, operation, and problems, issues, and concerns (1996, p. 90). As Stringer notes: "As participants work through these issues, they will extend

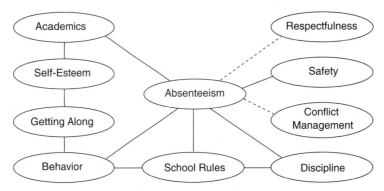

FIGURE 5-1   Eastview's Concept Map of the Factors Affecting Absenteeism

their understanding of the organization and aspects of its operation that are relevant to their problems, issues, and concerns" (1996, pp. 90–91). A review of the school, with these features in mind, may provide insight into the data you have collected.

Concept Mapping

Stringer (1996) suggests that concept maps are another useful strategy for action research participants to use to visualize the major influences that have affected the study. For example, what were the perspectives of the students? parents? teachers? administrators? A concept map gives participants an opportunity to display their analysis of the problem and to determine consistencies and inconsistencies that may exist between the disparate groups. For example, Jack Reston at Eastview Elementary School (see chapter 6) concluded that the following factors were major influences on the success of the school's absenteeism policy; respectfulness, safety, conflict management, discipline, school rules, behavior, getting along, self-esteem, and academics. Further, Jack believed that some relationships (real and perceived) existed between these factors (see Figure 5–1).

Analyze Antecedents and Consequences

Stringer (1996) also suggests a process of mapping antecedents (causes) and consequences (effects) to help action researchers identify the major elements of their analysis (p. 96). Using this framework provides a visual representation of the causal relationships that you the teacher researcher now believe exist. It is also helpful to revisit the causal relationships uncovered in your review of literature to determine challenges and support for your analysis and interpretations.

Displaying Findings

It is important to try to summarize the information you have collected in an appropriate and meaningful format that you can share with interested colleagues. To do this, it is helpful for teacher researchers to "think display" as they consider how to convey their findings to interested colleagues. You might use matrixes, charts, concept maps, graphs, and figures—whatever works as a practical way to encapsulate the findings of your study. I have also wit-

Data Analysis Techniques
_____ Identify themes.
_____ Code surveys, interviews, and questionnaires.
_____ Ask key questions: who, what, where, when, why, and how?
_____ Do an organizational review of the school.
_____ Develop a concept map.
_____ Analyze antecedents and consequences.
_____ Display findings.
_____ State what is missing.

nessed teacher researchers who have made excellent use of other audiovisual media such as videotape and computer multimedia presentations (incorporating text, charts, matrixes, audio, and video) to represent their findings. These visual displays of data serve an important function for teachers who wish to share findings and celebrate their insights in a public forum (see chapter 6 for further discussion). Putting your data into a visual format might also help you "see" new aspects of your data!

State What's Missing

Finally, as part of your full reporting, flag for the consumers of your research what pieces of the puzzle are still missing and identify what questions remain for which you have not been able to provide answers. Often we find ourselves wanting and needing to provide answers, to move beyond our data with unwarranted assertions that may, in some cases, ultimately lead to embarrassing questions about what we actually did! In keeping with the theme of avoiding premature judgment (arriving at answers to problems without systematic inquiry), the data analysis technique of stating what's missing allows you to hint at what might/should be done next in your quest to better understand the findings of your study. (See Research in Action Checklist 5–1 for a list of data analysis techniques.)

Data Interpretation Techniques

You may wonder, why bother with interpretation, especially since interpretation involves taking risks and making educated guesses that might be off-base? Wolcott believes that qualitative (action) researchers must accept "the risks and challenges of the interpretive mode" because in doing so we can "demonstrate to others (and reassure ourselves) that, in spite of their undistinguished origins, our works and the implications to be drawn from them are socially significant" (Wolcott, 1994, p. 258). In other words, Wolcott argues for the importance of interpretation because as teacher researchers, our interpretations matter to the lives of our students. In addition, the process of interpretation is important because it can challenge teacher researchers' taken-for-granted assumptions and beliefs about the educational processes they have investigated.

The list of techniques for data interpretation that follow are adapted from Wolcott (1994, pp. 39–46) and Stringer (1996, pp. 87–96) but have been reframed to apply specifically to teacher researchers.

Extend the Analysis

One technique that is low on the data interpretation risk scale is to simply extend the analysis of your data by raising questions about the study, noting implications that *might* be drawn without actually drawing them. As Wolcott suggests, "This is a strategy for *pointing* the way rather than *leading* the way" (1994, p. 40, italics added). For example, "While it appears as though the teen theater improvisation model positively impacts audience participation, a number of questions are raised by this strategy." In this example from Cathy Mitchell's Teen Theater group's use of improvisation, the analysis of data can be extended by raising questions about the intervention that were not asked as part of the original investigation, but which may signal the beginning of the next action research cycle.

Similarly, in the Highland Park High School vignette, the research raised questions such as, Is the total elimination of letter and number grades the best way to deemphasize grades? Is there a way to deemphasize grades that requires less paperwork on the teacher's part? What is an appropriate role for students to play in determining their own grades? How can grades be deemphasized while teachers still maintain very specific criteria/outcomes for students?

Connect Findings with Personal Experience

Action research is very personal business, so it makes sense to personalize our interpretations. For example, you may present your findings with the prelude: "Based on my experiences in conducting this study, this is what I make of it all." Remember, you know your study better than anyone else; after all, it's been conducted in your classroom or school and focused on your students. You have been there for every twist and turn along the way, trying to make sense of discrepant events just when you thought you "had it right." Share your interpretations based on your intimate knowledge and understandings of schools and classrooms and teaching and learning. For example, Deborah South had experienced the frustration of working with unmotivated children and the apparent futility of a study skills intervention. When faced with the "So what?" question, she based her interpretation not only on the analysis of data (test scores, surveys, interviews, and observations) but also on the memories and emotions of adolescent off-task behavior—a powerful interpretive lens.

Seek the Advice of "Critical" Friends

If you have difficulty focusing an interpretive lens on your work, rely on your trusted colleagues to offer insights that you may have missed because of your closeness to the work. Offer your accounts to colleagues with the request that they share with you their possible interpretations. For example, the group of teachers at Highland Park High School found that their interpretations were enriched by the multiple viewpoints that came as a result of their collaboration. Remember, these colleagues may be people you have never met face-to-face but with whom you have talked in action research chat rooms on the Internet. Similarly, you may ask your informants (students, parents, teachers, and administrators) for their insights.

But beware! The more opinions you seek the more you will receive, and often these suggestions come with the expectation that you will accept the advice! Over time you will develop reciprocity with a cadre of trusted, like-minded colleagues who will selflessly fulfill the role of a critical friend. Take the time to build these relationships and reap the rewards they offer. For example, when Deborah South concluded from her data analysis and interpretation that her study skills class was the "cause" of her students' lack of motivation, her critical friends in her action research class protested that interpretation and provided her with ideas for alternate explanations. What Deborah gained from the feedback of her critical friends was a commitment to change the "intervention" that was being touted as "the solution" to the "unmotivated students" problem in the school.

Contextualize Findings in the Literature

Uncovering external sources as part of the review of related literature is a powerful way for teacher researchers to provide support for the study's findings. Wolcott (1994) suggests that qualitative (action) researchers "draw connections with external authority. Most often this is accomplished through informed references to some recognized body of theory in one's special field, or to the recognized classics, in the tradition of the literature review" (p. 34). Making these connections also provides teacher researchers with a way to share with colleagues the existing knowledge base in a specific area of focus and to acknowledge the unique contribution the teacher researcher has made to our understanding of the topic studied.

Turn to Theory

Let me offer a modest definition of **theory** as "an analytical and interpretive framework that helps the researcher make sense of 'what is going on' in the social setting being studied" (Mills, 1993, p.103). Theory serves a number of important roles for qualitative (action) researchers.

First, theory provides a way for teacher researchers to link their work to broader issues of the day. As Wolcott suggests, "One interpretive tack is to examine a case in terms of competing theories and then proclaim a winner or, more often, attempt some eclectic resolution" (1994, p. 43). Second, "theory allows the researcher to search for increasing levels of abstraction, to move beyond a purely descriptive account." That level of abstraction "allow(s) us to communicate the essence of descriptive work to our colleagues at research meetings" (Mills, 1993, p. 115). Lastly, theory can provide a rationale or sense of meaning to the work we do. As educators we have all been influenced by learning theories that provide a safe haven for our own work. Share the theories that appear to help make sense of your data.

For example, Clem Annice's story of the use of technology to enhance mathematics learning for the students at Billabong Elementary School (chapter 4), is influenced by theories about how students best learn math. Some of these theories are evident in the references to how students were using technology for "drill-and-kill" activities and how access to calculators was limited because calculator functions had been removed from the computers. The vignette suggests that other theories explain how students best learn math by challenging the "rote learning" theory that appeared well established at Billabong Elementary.

Know When to Say "When"!

Finally, if you don't feel comfortable with offering an interpretation, don't do it. Be satisfied with suggesting what needs to be done next and use that as a starting point for the next action research cycle. Restate the problem as you now see it and explain how you think

Data Interpretation Techniques

_____ Extend the analysis by raising questions.
_____ Connect the findings with personal experience.
_____ Seek the advice of critical friends.
_____ Contextualize findings in the literature.
_____ Turn to theory.

you will fine-tune your efforts as you strive to increase your understanding of the phenomenon you have investigated. As Wolcott cautions, "don't detract from what you have accomplished by tacking on a wimpy interpretation" (1994, p. 41). (See Research in Action Checklist 5–2 for a list of data interpretation techniques.)

Sharing Your Interpretations Wisely

As educators we have all, at some time, been exposed to what are variously called "fads," "the pendulum swing," the "bandwagon," and so on. As such, many of us may hesitate to embrace anything new or different that comes our way in schools, calming ourselves with the mantra "This, too, shall pass!" If we as professional educators attempt to use our action research findings only as a soapbox from which we simply have sought findings to confirm our beliefs and values, then we risk being alienated by our colleagues. Avoid being evangelical about your interpretations, connect them closely to your data and analysis, and share your newfound understandings with colleagues in an appropriate manner.

Count What Counts! Using Descriptive Statistics

Data analysis and interpretation can also involve the use of descriptive statistics to help make sense of your findings. My advice here is simple: Count what counts! If it makes sense to tally and count events, categories, occurrences, test scores, and the like, use an appropriate descriptive statistic. Do not feel compelled to include elaborate statistical measures simply to add a perceived sense of rigor or credibility to your inquiry. Recall from chapter 1 that action research is a very different kind of inquiry than traditional research and as such is less interested in the claims that scientists use statistics to make. Treat descriptive statistics as one of an array of many useful tools that can help teacher researchers gain insight into their data and communicate it efficiently to others.

In the following sections of this chapter, we will very briefly discuss measures of central tendency (mean, mode, and median) and variability (standard deviation). For a more detailed explanation of the appropriate use of these statistics, I recommend Vockel and Asher, 1996, and Witte, 1985. Many readily available computer programs, such as SPSSX and StatView, may be accessible for computing statistics at your school or university. Remember, you also have many excellent math specialists in your school or district, so don't hesitate to call on those resources with questions.

Why Use Descriptive Statistics

Descriptive statistics give us a shorthand way of giving lots of information about a range of numbers using only one or two numbers. For example, in chapter 3 we discussed the use of attitude scales (Likert Scales and Semantic Differentials) to measure students' attitudes. One way to provide a great deal of information about our students' attitudes (as measured by these instruments) is to use descriptive statistics to *describe* the students' attitudes. For example, we might describe students' attitudes to a new mathematics curriculum (see chapter 3) by reporting the average response to the following item on a questionnaire:

1. I believe that the problem-solving skills I learn in class help me make good problem solving decisions outside of school.

    SA   A   U   D   SD

By assigning the following point values; SA = 5, A = 4, U = 3, D = 2, SD = 1, and calculating the average response, we would be able to describe, on average, what children believed about the transfer of problem-solving skills to decisions outside of school. In other words, the use of a number, in this case an average, conveys a great deal of information about students' attitudes and helps us make sense of our questionnaire data. Without the use of numbers we would be limited to talking about an individual student's response to each question and not in more general terms about the attitudes of all of our students.

Measures of Central Tendency

Simply put, a measure of central tendency is a single number that gives us information about the entire group of numbers we are examining. Three common measures of central tendency are the *mean* (the average), the *mode* (the most frequently occurring score/s), and the *median* (the middle score). In education, perhaps the most common descriptive statistic used by teachers is the mean. It allows us to talk in generalities and to compare how the students in our class have performed "on average" in comparison to other students or over a given time period. As teachers you have no doubt calculated many averages, but remember:

The **mean** is calculated by adding together all of the scores (observations) and dividing by the number of scores.

Mean = The sum of all the scores divided by the number of scores.

For example, you administer a mathematics test with 100 questions to the thirty students in your class. After grading the tests, you award the following scores: 95, 95, 92, 92, 90, 90, 90, 88, 88, 85, 85, 85, 82, 82, 82, 82, 79, 79, 75, 75, 75, 75, 75, 72, 72, 72, 69, 69, 69, 65.

$$\text{Mean } (\overline{X}) = \frac{\Sigma X \text{ (the sum of the scores)}}{n \text{ (the number of scores)}}$$

$$= \frac{2{,}424}{30}$$

$$= 80.8$$

The mean is greatly affected by extreme scores, since it is "pulled" in the direction of the atypical values. For that reason, the median is sometimes a better descriptor of the full range of scores. For the most part, though, the mean (or the average) is the easiest, most familiar measure to use.

The **median** is the middle score in a distribution when the scores are ordered from the highest to the lowest. If there is an odd number of scores (say 31), then the middle score (the 16th one) is the median. But in the distribution of math scores above, there is an even number of scores. To find the midpoint in the distribution when there is an even number of scores, we must add the two middle scores in the rank-ordered distribution and divide by two. In this case we would add together the two scores that are at positions 15 and 16. In this case it would be scores 82 and 82. Therefore, 82 is the median score.

The **mode** is the most frequently occurring score in a distribution. In the case of these math scores, the mode would be 75, because that score was received by five students in the class. A distribution of scores can have more than one mode (making it bi-modal or multimodal) or have no mode at all. The mode is the least useful measure of central tendency: It tells us only about the score received most often and doesn't give us any information about the other scores.

Measure of Variability: The Standard Deviation

As teachers, we may have been exposed to standard deviations but perhaps did not fully understood its meaning. For example, we may have received test scores for our students following administration of a standardized test with individual scores, a class average, and a standard deviation. For our purposes, it is not important to see and memorize the formula for the standard deviation or even to know its origins. It is more important to understand the concepts of variability and standard deviation, to know what they mean and when they would be appropriate to use.

A measure of variability tells us "how spread out a group of scores are" (Gay, 1996, p. 432). The standard deviation is the most important measure of variability for our action research purposes. While the mean is a measure of a position in a distribution of scores (in this case, 80.8 on a scale of 1–100), the standard deviation is a measure of distance from that mean (Witte, 1985, pp. 53–56). In essence, the standard deviation helps us understand approximately how much a particular score deviates from the average score.

Used in conjunction, the mean and standard deviation can provide you and your colleagues with a great deal of information about the data you have collected if you have determined that it is data that can be counted. See Key Concepts Box 5–1 for some of the uses of descriptive statistics.

Be Careful About Your Claims

A final caveat: Be careful about how you "interpret" the descriptive statistics that you use to analyze your data and be careful about the claims you make based on the use of a descriptive statistical analysis. Be clear about the limited significance that can be attached to averages and standard deviations. Remember that these statistics are used for description, not for identifying statistically significant relationships that can be generalized to the larger population.

KEY CONCEPTS BOX 5–1

Descriptive Statistics	
DEFINITION OF MEASURE	**TYPE USED IN ACTION RESEARCH**
A **measure of central tendency** is a single number that gives us information about an entire group of numbers.	• Mean (the average) • Mode (the most frequently occurring score/s) • Median (the middle score)
A **measure of variability** tells us how spread out a group of scores are.	• Standard deviation (a measure of distance from the mean that helps us understand approximately how much a *particular* score deviates from the *average* score)

Clearly, this discussion about descriptive statistics is quite brief. My experiences with teacher researchers is that, like me, they are somewhat math phobic and reluctant to incorporate statistics into their studies. But as Pelto and Pelto (1978) remind us:

In fact, not only humans but also other animals are constantly counting things in the process of adapting to their environments. Basic processes of learning, as described by experimental psychologists, most often imply some kind of counting or measurement that permits an animal (human or other) to distinguish between one condition and another as a relevant stimulus for appropriate action. (p. 123)

If counting things positively contributes to understanding your research or suggests a relationship that warrants further investigation, then consider the use of whatever statistic is most appropriate. And, if you are math phobic but still want to examine whether statistics can give you insight into your data, do not hesitate to call on the skills of your critical friends and colleagues.

Summary

This chapter has explained the concepts of and provided techniques for data analysis and data interpretation. Data analysis is undertaken when researchers want to summarize and represent data that have been collected in a dependable, accurate, reliable, correct, and right manner. Researchers interpret data to make sense of the research findings, to answer the question "So what?"

Data analysis techniques included identifying themes; coding surveys, interviews and questionnaires; asking key questions; doing an organizational review; concept mapping; undertaking problem analysis of antecedents and consequences; and displaying findings.

Data interpretation techniques included extending the analysis by raising questions; connecting findings with personal experience; seeking the advice of critical friends; contextualizing findings in the literature; and turning to theory.

Finally, we briefly defined descriptive statistical techniques that can be used in the analysis, interpretation, and presentation of data. A measure of central tendency is a single number that gives us information about an entire group of numbers. The three most common measures of central tendency are the mean (the average), the mode (the most frequently occurring score/s), and the median (the middle score). A measure of variability tells us how spread out a group of scores are. The standard deviation is a measure of distance from the mean that helps us understand approximately how much a particular score deviates from the average score.

For Further Thought

1. How will you analyze each data source that you have indicated in your data collection plan? Remember: Don't collect data when you don't know what you are going to do with it.
2. How would you distinguish between data analysis and data interpretation?
3. What descriptive statistics make sense for you to use? What other help do you need with statistics? What statistics software do you have access to?

CHAPTER 6

Action Planning for Educational Change

This chapter discusses different steps in action planning that help ensure teacher researchers are able to implement positive educational change based on the insights they gain through action research. **Action planning** basically attempts to answer the question, "Based on what I have learned from my research, what should I do now?"

A Steps to Action Chart is presented to guide teacher researchers through the action planning process. The chart identifies the findings of the study, the recommended action that targets a given finding, who is responsible for specific actions, who needs to be consulted or informed about the findings of the study and the concomitant actions, how to monitor the effects of your actions through the collection of data, a timeline for when the actions and monitoring will occur, and any resources that will be needed to carry out the action.

Finally, this chapter will discuss action planning within the context of challenges that face the teacher researcher and the conditions under which action research and the educational change that follows it can occur.

After reading this chapter you should be able to

1. Complete an action plan by working through a Steps to Action Chart.
2. Become aware of challenges that confront the action researcher in the action planning process.

3. Become aware of conditions that facilitate educational change in school environments.

⚎

Reflecting on Admission Criteria
JACK RESTON

This vignette is the story of an elementary school principal who modeled the process of action research for his teachers, a number of whom were involved in their own action research projects at the same time. Jack's story is particularly powerful because it illustrates the willingness of a school principal to investigate the effect of a policy he had developed. Further, Jack tackled the difficult problem facing many teachers and principals: how to keep children in school and the importance of being in school. The result of the study was an action plan that required the change of a district-wide absenteeism policy.

I was selected to serve on a committee of administrators to review current policies concerning students' absenteeism. The task of the committee was to write a new student absenteeism policy, which led to the adoption of a new absenteeism policy and procedure. I recognized throughout this process a need to look into student absenteeism with more depth and understanding, and for this reason I selected the topic of student absenteeism for my action research project.

I initiated my research project with a review of our school's attendance rate profile for the last five years. The profile showed little or no change in the attendance rate. This was a concern because I cross-referenced the attendance rate with the funds allocated for various attendance incentives designed to motivate students and could easily see that the dollars spent on incentives were not affecting the attendance rate. I sat at my desk and thought about all my current and past efforts. It was clear that I was not truly passionate about student absenteeism. I had never taken time to clearly understand its causes or researched the best solutions to prevent it. I was passionate about my belief that a child's success in life depends on a solid educational foundation. I was passionate about my belief that students cannot afford to miss class at any time. I was passionate about my belief that absenteeism is a symptom or gauge of a student experiencing failure in school.

I began by asking three questions:

1. What student characteristics are associated with student absenteeism?
2. What are some longitudinal effects of student absenteeism?
3. What are some effective strategies to prevent student absenteeism?

I reviewed current studies, literature, local and national profiles, written surveys, and interviews. I found that absenteeism was highly associated with dropping out of school, academic failure, and delinquency. I learned what students and parents in our school believed about the relationship between school and absenteeism. I concluded that I really did not understand the belief systems of families at risk of poor attendance in school. I conducted a massive survey of students and parents within a four-day period of time. Surveys gathered data concerning such things as respectfulness of students, safety in school, conflict management, discipline, school rules, self-esteem, and academics. In addition, the survey gathered data on mobility rates, volunteerism, and levels of education in parents. The identity of the families surveyed was kept unknown. Instead, the surveys were coded as "at risk" or "not at risk" data.

I collected data from the surveys in three stages. First, each family in the school was mailed a survey. The surveys arrived at the homes of students on a Saturday. Completed surveys were returned to the school prior to 9:00 A.M. on the Monday. Second, each student in the entire school was surveyed in their classrooms at 9:00 A.M. on the Monday. Third, selected students and parents were interviewed between Monday and Tuesday to collect data similarly gathered on the surveys.

Student teachers from a nearby university and local educators with experience in action research interviewed selected students and parents. The interviews were conducted over the telephone or face to face. I compiled all of the data and began searching for a better understanding of at-risk students and parents at my school. I found these people believed the following:

- Other students did not respect them.
- They did not use conflict management skills.
- Adults in the school did not handle discipline effectively.
- School rules are not fair.
- There are behavior problems associated with this group.
- At-risk students perform poorly in academic areas.
- At-risk students in this school are not motivated by rewards such as drawings for prizes and certificates.

This information led to major changes in our approach to improving attendance in school. First, we stopped spending large sums of money for rewards and drawings. Although these are nice things for students, they are ineffective in dealing with the problem of poor attendance. Second, we recognized punitive measures were having little effect on attendance. This led us to the belief that students succeeding in school were more likely to attend school regularly.

We began a concentrated effort to improve the success of students at school both academically and emo-tionally. This included the use of student/parent/teacher/principal contracts, daily planners for students, individual conferences between the student and the principal every fourteen days to review grades and behaviors, better assessments to locate students having academic problems, improved instructional techniques and alignment of curriculum, and more concentrated efforts to improve the self-esteem of students.

In conclusion, I found the following to be true in our effort to improve student absenteeism:

1. Students need to be successful in school.
2. Students need to be connected to the school.
3. Students need friendships with students and adults at school.
4. Students need to develop the skills to deal with life's daily anxieties.
5. The school needs to develop meaningful relationships with the family.

Based on these learnings, I worked with teachers and parents to develop quick responses that unite the student, parent, educator, and community in a preventive effort to minimize absenteeism.

To support Kurt Lewin's prophetic statement, "No action without research; no research without action" (as cited by Adelman, 1993, p. 8), this chapter discusses how teacher researchers can ensure that action is a natural outcome of their action research efforts. Without action, we have done nothing more than replicate what we set out to avoid—doing research *on* someone for our own benefit, whatever that may be. But the reward for us all in this process is taking action to improve the educational experiences of our children—action is at the very heart of the action research endeavor.

In Jack Reston's vignette we see a principal and members of the school community (children, parents, teachers, student teachers) who persevered in trying to solve an important problem that faces many schools—how to keep children in school. Reston's action plan identified a number of actions targeted to the findings of the study: developing students' skills to deal with the anxieties of life and school, developing strategies to ensure student success in school, developing meaningful relationships with families, improved instructional techniques and curriculum alignment, strategies to develop meaningful relationships/partnerships with families, and so on. In the action planning process, Reston had reflected on the findings of the study and what he now understood about the problem of absenteeism. As a result of this reflection, he was better able to plan the next steps in the action research process.

Action planning is a natural next step in the action research process. Using the guidelines in this chapter, you will be able to ensure that the necessary steps are taken to bring your efforts to fruition.

Developing Action Plans

At this phase of the action research process, the teacher researcher is basically trying to answer the following question, "Based on what I have learned from this investigation, what should I do now?" At this point, teacher researchers should reflect on the taken-for-granted assumptions that guided them to the investigation in the first instance and determine what course of action to take next. This reflection allows time for both teachers and administrators to determine what they have learned from their investigations and the related professional literature and to decide on the necessary steps to action.

To facilitate this process consider the use of a Steps to Action Chart similar to the ones shown in Tables 6–1 and 6–2. (Table 6–1 shows a generic Steps to Action Chart; Table 6–2 shows the Steps to Action Chart created by Jack Reston for his study of student absenteeism.) By working through the steps included on the chart, teacher researchers will have a list of

- What they learned (findings).
- The recommended actions that target a given finding.
- Who is responsible for specific actions (responsibility).
- Who needs to be consulted or informed about the findings of the study and the associated actions.
- Who will monitor or collect the effects of actions.
- Dates when the actions and monitoring will occur.
- Any resources that will be needed to carry out the action.

Elements of this chart will look familiar to you. Monitoring and data collection efforts will once again involve you in the action research process. In each case you will focus on a new problem such as "What are the effects of this action on student performance?" and develop specific data collection/monitoring techniques to answer the question. Although not included on the chart, the monitoring/data collection techniques (see chapter 3) would lead to data analysis and interpretation (see chapter 5) with findings and further steps to action. Hence the cycle repeats itself again and again. It may be that you are entirely satisfied with an intervention and that the proposed action is to continue with its implementation. This routinization of instruction still suggests that as a reflective teacher you will continue to collect data—to monitor the effects of your instruction on your students' performance and attitude. At that point, as a self-renewing school faculty or as an individual teacher with a reflective professional disposition, you will continue your systematic inquiry into some other aspect of your practice. (See Research in Action Checklist 6–1 for a list of steps to action.)

Levels of Action Planning

Action planning can occur at a number of different levels within the school: *individual*, *team*, and *schoolwide* depending on the scope of the action research effort. It is also possible that action planning may take place at a number of these different levels during a

TABLE 6–1 Steps To Action Chart

Summary of Findings Research Questions	Recommended Action Targeted to Findings	Who Is Responsible for the Action?	Who Needs To Be Consulted or Informed?	Who Will Monitor/ Collect Data?	Timeline	Resources
1.0 Research question #1					When will action/ monitoring occur?	What will you need in order to carry out your action?
1.1 Finding #1 1.2 Finding #2		• Teacher • Team	• Teacher • Team			
2.0 Research question #2		• Department head • Principal • Parents • Students	• Department head • Principal • Parents • Students			
2.1 Finding #1 2.2 Finding #2 2.3 etc.						

TABLE 6-2 Jack Reston's Steps to Action Chart

Summary of Findings Research Questions	Recommended Action Targeted to Findings	Who Is Responsible for the Action? T – Teacher S – Student P – Princpal PA – Parent/s	Who Needs To Be Consulted or Informed?	Who Will Monitor/ Collect Data?	Timeline	Resources
1.0 What student characteristics are attributed to student absenteeism? 1.1 Lack of respect 1.2 Poor conflict management skills 1.3 Lack of self-discipline 1.4 Behavior problems 1.5 Poor academic performance	1.1 Model respect for others. 1.2–1.4 Develop skills to deal with life's daily anxieties. 1.5 Improve strategies to develop success in school.	1.1 T, S, P 1.2–1.4 T, S, P, Pa 1.5 T, P	1.2–1.4 Pa	T, P: 1. Observations 2. Intentions 3. Surveys 4. Test data	Ongoing throughout school year.	None
2.0 What are some longitudinal effects of student absenteeism? 2.1 Dropouts 2.2 Academic failure 2.3 Delinquency	2.1–2.3 Students need to be connected to school. Develop strategies to build a sense of "belonging" at school.	2.1–2.3 T, P. S		T, P: 1. Observations 2. Intentions 3. Surveys 4. Test data	Ongoing throughout school year.	None

3.0 What are some effective strategies to prevent student absenteeism?				T, P: 1. Observations 2. Intentions 3. Surveys 4. Test data	Ongoing throughout school year.	
3.1 Student/Parent/Teacher/Principal contracts	3.1 Implement contracts.	3.1 S, Pa, T, P	3.1 S, Pa			
3.2 Daily planners	3.2 Purchase & use planners.	3.2 P				3.2 $'s for planners
3.3 Diagnostic tools	3.3 Work with district office to administer diagnostic tests.	3.3 P	3.3 District office			
3.4 Self-esteem strategies	3.4 Implement self-esteem curriculum.	3.4 T				
3.5 Improved teaching & curriculum	3.5 Encourage ongoing professional development.	3.5 T, P				3.5 $'s for P.D.

Steps to Action
_____ Findings of the research.
_____ Recommended action.
_____ Responsibilities.
_____ Sharing findings with colleagues.
_____ Ongoing monitoring (data collection).
_____ Timeline for action.
_____ Resources.

single investigation. For example, the problem under investigation may have had a school-wide focus such as to determine the effects of an innovative reading curriculum (with an emphasis on constructing meaning) on student performance (as measured by statewide assessment scores and monthly criterion-referenced tests). Participation in the schoolwide effort also necessitated that teachers meet in grade-level teams to plan appropriate reading interventions and to analyze regularly collected data. Finally, individual teachers had to adapt the intervention as appropriate for their own students' needs. In this case, action planning was undertaken at all levels within the school.

Individual

Typically, **individual action planning** will be characterized by teacher researchers who have worked through an action research cycle, either as part of a course, licensure, or grant requirement or by teacher researchers who are undertaking action research as a regular component of their practice. Individual teachers can still work through the Steps to Action Chart (see Table 6-1) and in so doing remind themselves of the steps that need to be taken to implement action and monitor the effects of the action. While the primary audience for the findings from the study is the individual teacher, it is important for teacher researchers to tap into the kind of support networks one will find at universities. As Elliott suggests:

> a small band of isolated teacher researchers can tap into a reflective counter culture in the form of an action-research network which transcends school boundaries and is linked to a teacher education institution. Membership of such a network can provide the kind of cultural resources which strengthen the capacity of aspiring teacher researchers to resist the time pressures operating on them from inside schools. (1991, pp. 66–67)

As discussed later, in chapter 8, this networking cannot only transcend school boundaries, it can transcend global boundaries via participation in on-line action research listservs and chat rooms. This kind of cyberspace network can strengthen the resolve of teachers who must work in isolation to continue with the process through the action planning stage and into the next revolution of the cycle.

Team

In an era of devolution of authority to schools to make decisions about appropriate curriculum and instruction and school-based decision making through "site councils," it is common to see teams of teachers, administrators, and sometimes parents working collaboratively on action research projects. Often these groups grow out of networks developed in an action research course among teachers with similar areas of interest and expertise. At other times they grow out of grant requirements for grade-level or discipline-based teams to work collaboratively on a school improvement focus. Regardless of the catalyst for the network, these **teams** all share a common focus at this stage in the action research process—to mobilize their collective energies to move forward with action. This process can be facilitated by working through the Steps to Action Chart and collaboratively determining who has responsibility for what, when, and where. Resolution of any issues that emerge at this stage is critical to the continued success and longevity of the action research team. At this stage the primary audience for the action plan is the team members. However, it is important for action research teams to seek appropriate ways to transcend the traditional boundaries that have historically seen small teams of teachers burn out without feedback and support from the environments in which they work.

Schoolwide

Schoolwide action research, as the name implies, is about all of the members of the school community working together with a single goal in mind. For example, a schoolwide emphasis on improving reading, writing, or math is a common area of focus in elementary schools. Similarly, and sadly, it is not uncommon to see a high school focus on the effects of a drug and alcohol curriculum on student attitude, understanding, and levels of use. However, the distinguishing feature in these examples is that they have been agreed on by the whole school faculty as the focus for a schoolwide school improvement effort that will be driven by the findings of an action research effort. Cooperation, collaboration, and communication are no less important in the action planning phase than they were during the other steps of the process.

The challenge at the schoolwide level is how to actively engage all of the participants in goal setting that is integral to the action planning process. There will always be finger pointing and denial, and it will take a skilled facilitator to move a faculty through the Steps to Action Chart if progress is to be made. Do not underestimate the necessity of meaningfully engaging all of the school community in this action planning process, or you will risk perpetual isolation in the world of playground supervision—been there, done that, bought the umbrella!

Action Should Be Ongoing

This discussion about action planning is not meant to suggest that action occurs only at the end of the action research process. The very dynamic nature of teaching necessitates that teachers make many changes to instruction during the course of a day based on the formative feedback (data) collected as an integral part of the teaching process. For example, preservice teachers are often requested to include on lesson plans "Evaluation" statements to the effect of "How will you know if your students have achieved your instructional objectives?" In other words, what data will you collect that informs your post-planning at the end of the day? Often this data is collected intuitively and informally in noninvasive ways. It is such a normative aspect of teaching that we take it for granted. As teachers we have been programmed to collect, analyze, and interpret data quickly and efficiently so we can suggest "findings" and take necessary "actions" (remediation, reteaching, related material, extension activities) that enable learning to proceed in a connected fashion.

The Importance of Reflection

Action planning is also a time for reflection—reflection on where you have been, what you have learned, and where you are going. Action planning and reflection give you an opportunity to identify your individual or collective continuing professional development needs. This reflection is facilitated by the review of the the related literature you collected early in the action research process in concert with your own findings. The following questions may also be helpful prompts for reflection:

- What were the intended and unintended effects of your actions?
- What educational issues arise from what you've learned about your practice?

Clearly, these are not questions that elicit quick and easy responses. They urge you to look back at your practice from the enlightened viewpoint of someone who has systematically inquired into the effects of teaching on student outcomes. In undertaking such reflection, you will position yourself to act responsively to the findings of your study. The remaining sections of this chapter will help you to further identify challenges you may face when attempting to implement change and will guide you in meeting those challenges and effecting positive educational change in your school.

Some Challenges Facing Teacher Researchers

As you reflect on the critical steps to action, it is important to consider the challenges that all teacher researchers face both when doing action research and attempting to effect educational change based on the results of their inquiry. If indeed we are going to avoid living out Sarason's prophecy of "the more things change, the more they will remain the same" (1990, p. 5), we must be prepared to address these obstacles. These hurdles include a lack of resources, resistance to change, reluctance to interfere with others' professional practices, reluctance to admit difficult truths, the challenge of finding a forum to share what you have learned, and the difficulty of making time for action research endeavors.

Lack of Resources

The scarcity of resources is perhaps the greatest obstacle to action planning you will face. Many excellent action research and change efforts have been blocked by the lack of resources and materials to use in the classroom. But by being innovative and remaining energized by what you have learned about your practice, you will find ways to make change happen. This may mean using creativity to solve materials management issues. Don't wait for an administrator, central office person, or philanthropist to offer what you need to be successful. Go after the grants, however small, to fund the resources you identify as critical to the success of your intervention. Use the data you have collected, analyzed, and interpreted as a way to build a case for resources that may be presented to Parent-Teacher Associations, district-wide committees, school boards, granting agencies, and so on, to make a case for what you need.

Action researchers also need professional as well as material resources. If action research is to become a part of your professional disposition and be continued over time, it must benefit both your own continued professional development and student outcomes. Identification of promising practices will suggest the kinds of professional development you need to seek, either individually or collectively. If your local university or school district can't provide the professional development you seek, use the Internet to find out who does. Again, use your findings to make a compelling, persuasive case for the kind of professional development you need—not what someone else thinks you need.

Resistance to Change

Any type of change, however small, may be viewed as threatening by some. After all, the status quo is familiar and comfortable. But the era of schools that refuse to innovate is past. The ever-changing social and political environment in which we live necessitates that teachers become sophisticated instructional leaders and decision makers who have the skills to empower students and other individuals in their learning communities. Participation in and support of the action research process is critical if there is to be a shift in the culture of schools to the reflective practitioner culture of the self-renewing school. Living the commitment to a dynamic school culture as opposed to living the traditional "advocate of constraint" persona will go a long way toward revitalizing an individual school's culture and bringing about positive change.

For example, Jack Reston's investigation of the effect of the school/district policy on absenteeism showed that attendance rates had remained the same in spite of costly student incentives that were an integral part of the policy. Once he realized that the current intervention was having no impact, James Reston knew he had to take responsibility for trying to change the system to make Eastview Elementary School an environment where all children (especially those at-risk for absenteeism) would want to come to school. That meant changing even fundamental things, such as the way administrators interacted with students and the amount of time he spent with them individually. In doing so, he overcame several factors, including the institutional resistance to change.

Reluctance to Interfere with Others' Professional Practices

Unfortunately, there seems to be a prevailing cultural value in schools of "don't mess around in someone else's professional practice"—especially if you are not invited. The dilemma here for the teacher researcher arises from a conflict between the desire to persuade colleagues to experiment with or embrace new practices that have been shown via action research to have positive effects and a "respect for the professional expertise of colleagues and their right to exercise authority within the confines of their own classroom" (Elliott, 1991, p. 59).

Often teacher researchers faced with this dilemma back away from their investigations and change efforts to "keep the peace" with colleagues. However, if we are to learn from our own and others' professional practice, we must be willing to set aside the traditional protection of each other's classrooms and to embrace as a community of learners the proposed action plan that emerges from our research.

How you approach this professional collaboration with other teachers in your school is as important as trying it at all. It is critical to the success of your action research and change efforts, particularly at the schoolwide level, not to have alienated yourself from others by appearing to be a member of some "enlightened elite" who now knows all of the answers to the problems that affect students' inability to do well on statewide assessments! You will have gone a long way to revitalizing the professional disposition of teaching if you have been able to nurture your own and your colleagues' understanding of the problems you have investigated and built a teamwide commitment to implementing action based on your findings. Collaboration can help break down these stubborn professional barriers.

Reluctance to Admit Difficult Truths

If we view action research and action planning as one way to empower teachers, we should also be aware of the increased accountability these efforts place on teacher researchers. We can't have it both ways: If we want the authority to make the changes we have recommended based on our action research findings, we must be prepared to look into the mirror and face what we see. After all, if each of us has the power to make the most important decisions in our schools—that is, the ones that have the greatest impact on students—then we must also not abdicate responsibility when things don't go our way. If what we learn is that, in spite of our best efforts and intentions, our interventions have not succeeded, we must be prepared to look objectively at the data and make new recommendations for change in our quest to provide the best education possible for our students.

For example, Deborah South had hoped to find in her action research project that the group of "unmotivated" students in her study skills class would respond positively to her instruction and guidance. Instead she noticed an alarming and demoralizing trend: Students' grades were dropping. Deborah had to wrestle with this "difficult truth" and carefully consider her own responsibility for the students' performance before coming to a conclusion about the best way to effect change to benefit these "unmotivated" students.

Finding a Forum to Share What You Learned

The potential for an action plan to serve as the catalyst for reflective conversation between professionals is limitless. Elliott argues that such data sharing "promotes a reflective conversation and is at the heart of any transformation of the professional culture" (1991, p. 60). However, an open conversation about what the data from the study suggest (analysis and interpretation) and how these findings have been transformed into a proposed action plan will not always be an easy one.

What is needed is a forum (local, national, or global!) for teachers to share their accounts and a recognition by the profession that change-oriented action research is an important part of the professional competencies of being a teacher. For example, preservice teacher preparation programs are incorporating action research into the requirements of some preservice programs. Individual schools are providing teachers with opportunities to showcase their action research skills as part of an annual teacher evaluation cycle; state and federal grants incorporate action research as part of the instructional improvement cycle; school-based decision-making teams are embracing an action research model to guide their school improvement efforts; and state teacher licensing agencies are incorporating action research into continuing license renewal requirements.

Although teacher researchers have not typically published their findings, the sharing of teacher researchers' stories has also been facilitated by web-based action research sites.

There is now a global forum in which teachers can share their stories, the actions they have taken based on their research, and what they have learned in subsequent action research cycles. (These on-line journals include *Educational Action Research, Networks, Action Research International*, and *Action Research Electronic Reader.*) The sharing of action plans and what teacher researchers learn in the process is critical to the emerging teacher-as-researcher culture.

Making Time for Action Research Endeavors

We have already discussed the challenge of making time for action research in your busy daily schedule. Just when you thought the action research cycle was over and you are ready to return to "just teaching," you are thrust back into the process with further reflection about the actions suggested by the findings of your study and the who, what, and when of the next cycle.

"You mean I need to take more action and monitor its effects? But I don't have the time to do one more thing!" This exasperated call for putting the brakes on the process is not uncommon or unreasonable. By the time you have arrived at action planning, you may be all but spent and happy to claim that the status quo is working just fine. If you fall into this category of teacher, I would suggest that you follow your instincts. Allow yourself time to reflect and plan at a bearable pace. You are no good to the students in your care if you are burned out. (As the parent of a kindergarten age child, the last thing I want is a professional teacher all worn out from a year of doing action research!) The goal is to evolve to the point where action and research become a part of your professional life but not at the expense of the energy you need to be vital, creative, and exciting in your daily teaching. After all, if the action research process cannot be normative and undertaken without adversely affecting your primary focus of teaching children, then it *should not be done*.

If, on the other hand, you have arrived at the action planning phase with renewed energy and enthusiasm for your work, if you are committed to implementing a locally con-textualized innovation that you believe will contribute to the well-being of the students in your care, and if you have maintained a clear sense of direction, mission, and purpose, then move forward in the process and share your stories by whatever medium you can! It will be your stories of success and being a lifelong learner that will change the culture of teaching. These are intimate changes that cannot be forced on any of us from outside—they must come from the passion within.

Regardless of international, national, state, and local trends and initiatives, the individual teacher researcher's ability to resolve the issue of time constraints will ultimately determine whether action research is routinized into their classroom. However, if we as a profession cannot find time to do the work associated with it, action research will be discarded on the dust heap of other promising educational initiatives.

Facilitating Educational Change

The goal of action research is to enhance the lives of students and teachers through positive educational change. We have just discussed several common challenges that teachers face when attempting to effect educational change based on action research findings. In addition to being prepared to address those challenges, you can help create an environment that is conducive to change. The following are eight conditions that facilitate the process of educational change (adapted from Miller & Lieberman, 1988, Sarason, 1990, and Fullan, 1993).

Teachers and Administrators Need to Restructure Power and Authority Relationships

The first condition for fostering action research and encouraging educational change is that teachers and administrators need to restructure power and authority relationships. Power relationships in schools have the potential to empower or underpower action planning efforts. **Power** is not being used in a pejorative sense here—teacher researchers have the potential to harness the collective power of their colleagues, including administrators, to bring about meaningful change through a democratic, liberating, and life-enhancing process. For this to happen, participants in the action research process must be prepared to ask the hard questions related to implementing action based on the findings of the study: What is the recommended action? Who is responsible for doing what? Who needs to be consulted or informed? How will the effects of the implementation be monitored? When will tasks be completed? What resources are needed?

Asking these questions invariably leads to discussions about who has the final decision-making power in the school. In an era of school-based decision making, it is likely that a team of teachers, parents, students, and administrators will have the authority to answer action planning questions and to make decisions. However, whether or not your school has a professional or bureaucratic model of school-based decision making in place will determine the amount of influence you will have individually or as a team. According to Conley (1991), the bureaucratic model emphasizes the formal authority of administrators to delegate responsibilities to subordinates, to formulate rules to govern subordinate behavior, and to implement centralized control, planning, and decision making. In contrast, the professional model emphasizes the professional discretion and expertise of teachers in diagnosing and addressing student needs with an aim to provide teachers the rights they expect as professionals.

Power should be seen as an investment, not as a means of controlling people. "If we look at power this way, teachers and principals can hold leadership roles, and, working together, they can help the schools build a professional culture" (Lieberman, 1988, p. 653). This view emphasizes a reflective practitioner culture that empowers rather than underpowers teachers.

Deborah South was empowered, for example, to make changes to the study skills program for unmotivated students based on what she learned from her action research study. Jack Reston was empowered to change the absenteeism policy for his school and to recommend changes to the district's absenteeism policy based on his new understandings of what worked and didn't work for keeping children in school. Viewed in this way, power was an investment in the quality of the educational experiences of many children.

Both Top-Down and Bottom-Up Strategies of Change Can Work

In effecting educational change, both top-down and bottom-up strategies of change can work (Hord, Rutherford, Huling-Austin, & Hall, 1987). **Top-down strategies** can be thought of as changes that are mandated by school/district/state administrators without giving teachers an equal voice in the decision-making process (bureaucratic model). Alternatively,

bottom-up strategies can be thought of as change that is driven by teachers when given the authority to make decisions (professional model). The debate over whether top-down or bottom-up efforts at change produce the greatest effects has flourished for many years. Fullan (1993, p. 38) concludes, "What is required is a different two-way relationship of pressure, support and continuous negotiation" such as a continuous discourse between administrators and teachers involved in a collaborative action research project.

For example, the teachers at Highland Park High School worked collaboratively with the school's assistant principal and involved him in the team's action research activities. In this respect, there was obvious support from the school's administration for the action research effort. Alternatively, the teachers at Billabong Elementary School (chapter 4) were quite resentful that the principal had mandated a math text for the school without consulting teachers in the process.

Teachers Must Be Provided with Support

Additionally, teachers involved in change efforts brought about by action research must be provided with support. Support for teachers in their endeavors ideally would come from all quarters: students, other teachers, the school administration, the families of students enrolled, government officials, and so on. For example, Jack Reston's investigation into absenteeism could not have occurred had it not been for the support of the parents, teachers, and student teachers (who helped with interviews). Deborah South relied heavily on the emotional support of her critical friends in the action research class when she shared the analysis and interpretation of her study of unmotivated students.

Every Person Is a Change Agent

Both individual and collective efforts are critical to successful change, and every person has the potential to be a change agent. The action research vignettes in this book illustrate the potential for change to happen at the individual, team, and schoolwide levels. But perhaps the key point of all of these examples is that it took the desire of an individual teacher or principal to initiate the action research process and to effect positive educational change based on the findings. As Fullan (1993, p. 39) reminds us, "Each and every teacher has the responsibility to help create an organization capable of individual and collective inquiry and continuous renewal, or [change] will not happen."

Those Involved Must Recognize that Change Tends not to Be Neat, Linear, or Rational

Equally important, those involved in action research must recognize that change tends not to be neat, linear, or rational. Consider as an example the work of Cathy Mitchell and the Duct Tape Theatre Company. While Cathy was able to confirm that her objective of making teen theater a more meaningful experience was sound, she also recognized that the approach of interactive improvisation did not have the desired effects. The audience did not respond to the "Violence Improv" scene as she expected, and as a result her action research project did not provide her with the tidy solutions she hoped for. While recommitted to her goal, Cathy is still faced with figuring out new ways to make teen theater a more meaningful experience. For Cathy, the processes of action research and change will be recursive and cyclical.

Teacher Researchers Must Pay Attention to the Culture of the School

A sixth condition is that teacher researchers must pay attention to the culture of the school. Change efforts should always be viewed in the context of the culture of the school and classroom in which the action research effort is being conducted. For example, until Jack Reston investigated the effectiveness of his school's absenteeism policies, it was assumed that the current reward system of drawings and certificates was effective. Instead, he found that the reward system made no difference for at-risk students. As a result, he tried to isolate what intervention would make a difference to these children. He used surveys and interviews to attempt to thoroughly understand the culture, values, and belief systems of the families of children at risk for absenteeism. Based on his findings, he was able to recommend meaningful changes to the school's policy on absenteeism that specifically responded to the needs of this group, especially their need to feel connected to the school.

The Outcome of Any Change Effort Must Benefit Students

A somewhat obvious condition for doing action research and effecting educational change is that the outcome of any change effort must benefit students if it is to be continued. Action research can provide a method for recording, measuring, and analyzing the results of an educational practice or intervention. For example, the data collected by James Rockford in his study of the effectiveness of keyboarding software on the class word processing rate provided conclusive evidence that the keyboarding software being tested was very effective and that time spent on computers at schools was critical. This persuasive data gave James confidence in the benefits of this educational intervention and supported his recommendation that teachers take students to the computer lab every day, monitor keyboarding habits, and see that each student received a minimum of ten minutes of practice per day.

Being Hopeful Is a Critical Resource

Finally, being hopeful is a critical resource if teachers are to perform action research and stay the course of change. Recall the words of Cathy Mitchell, whose teen theater action research project was described in chapter 2:

> The most important part of this project is that I felt renewed energy for my work. Last year at this time I was busily seeking a replacement for myself and announcing to everyone that I wasn't going to direct teens anymore. I didn't even consider that there was a problem that could be addressed and remedied. It feels really good to expect something to happen in my working life as a result of the research and reflection that I myself have done.

As a result of her action research inquiry, Cathy has created a powerful resource for herself—the hope that she will discover new ways to make her work meaningful for teens. Even though she once felt like quitting, she writes that this new hope is powerful enough to sustain her through future change efforts.

For educational change to be successful, all those involved must be optimistic about the results of the transformation. (Of course, they also need to be realistic: Being hopeful is not the same as being naive.) Reform efforts can sometimes generate negative emotions and a sense of hopelessness because the individuals involved may be on the defensive from external attack or part of small groups of reformers suffering burnout (Fullan, 1997). But if we are going to make progress with reform efforts, we have to weather the negative emotions to succeed.

It is possible that at the action planning stage of the action research process you will again have to confront negative emotions from other stakeholders in the process. This is a critical turning point in the action research process: You can easily adopt the position that this is a lost cause, or you can rely on the most critical resource any of us have—*hope*. Individually, we all have to take a stand on whether our investigations have yielded findings that warrant taking action. If we have done a good job, we should have collected findings that are trustworthy and true. Reflect on the hope you felt when you first began your project. Then use that hope to sustain you through the action planning process. As Fullan argues, "Being hopeful and taking action in the face of important lost causes may be less emotionally draining than being in a permanent state of despair" (1997, pp. 231–32).

Recognize that we can do little to really change how a colleague thinks, acts, and feels—we must all answer to ourselves and the search for self-efficacy that comes with being a professional educator. If any of us reach a point in our professional lives when we feel that we can no longer make a difference or no longer struggle in the face of adversity (limited time or resources, for example) it is probably time to try another professional calling. In education, whether it's a lack of chalk, paper, or RAM for the computer, none of us have ever had a blank check to finance the time and resources we think we need to be the best we can be. But what sets us apart from other professionals is the belief that we can make a difference in children's lives, with or without the resources.

Schools are complex social settings, and those of us who have taught at a number of different schools know how schools can differ from community to community. You are in the best position to know what lessons you can apply from this broad discussion of educational change to your own situation. But we can all learn from each other's experience by sharing our stories. Whenever possible, share your action research stories with others. In doing so you will help revitalize the professional disposition of teachers.

What Do Teachers Gain Through All of This Work?

If you are now living this process, perhaps in a quiet, unassuming way, what follows will validate your work as a professional—contribute to your sense of self-efficacy—for it is within that we all find the rewards that teaching has to offer. If we return to our earlier discussion about critical/postmodern perspectives of action research, you will recall an emphasis on what we believe as a professional community and what we as individual teacher researchers have gained through all of this work that has systematically guided us to action.

Having invested a great deal of time and energy into investigating the taken-for-granted relationships and practices in your professional life, you have now arrived at the point where the "rubber meets the road." Will you really initiate action and continue the process? If you answer in the affirmative, you have gone a long way toward embracing some of the tenets of a socially responsive approach to research: You have engaged in a democratic process that has encouraged the participation of your colleagues. The process has been equitable with the participants all having one voice. The experience has been liberating and has freed you from accepting at blind faith something that may have been forced on you. Finally, the experience has been life enhancing for you as a professional and for the students who will benefit from your teaching.

For me, the ultimate pay-off for teacher researchers who have stuck with the process, learned and internalized the action research skills, and are now committed to action and self-renewal is the belief and knowledge that those who are the real benefactors of your work are the students in your care. There can be no argument against this powerful and altruistic goal.

Summary

Action planning is an effort to answer the question, "Based on what I have learned from my research, what should I do now?" This chapter has presented a Steps to Action Chart that addresses issues related to what teacher researchers have learned (findings), what recommended action targets a given finding, who is responsible for specific actions (responsibility), who needs to be consulted or informed about the findings of the study and the concomitant actions, how you will monitor the effect of your actions by collecting data, on what dates will the actions and monitoring occur, and what resources will be needed to carry out the action.

This chapter also discussed how to overcome the challenges faced by action researchers who seek to implement positive educational change: lack of resources; resistance to change; reluctance to interfere with others' professional practices; reluctance to admit difficult truths; difficulty of finding a forum to share what you have learned; and lack of time for action research endeavors.

This chapter also noted eight factors for facilitating change in a school environment: teachers and administrators need to restructure power relationships; both top-down and bottom-up strategies for change can work; teachers involved in change efforts brought about by action research must be provided with support; every person is a change agent; those involved must recognize that change tends not to be neat, linear, and rational; teacher researchers must pay attention to the culture of the school; the outcome of any change effort must be beneficial to be continued; and being hopeful is a powerful resource.

For Further Thought

1. Develop an action plan based on your action research findings and present it using the Steps to Action Chart format.
2. How would you apply what you have learned about the challenges of implementing educational change to overcome potential obstacles that you may encounter in taking action?

CHAPTER 7

Sharing, Critiquing, and Celebrating Action Research

While chapter 6 showed teacher researchers how to ensure that action is planned with consideration of the findings of the study and the potential obstacles to implementing change, this chapter addresses different ways of sharing action research, criteria for judging action research efforts, and the importance of celebrating our professional learnings.

This chapter addresses the benefits of sharing action research with others and discusses two alternatives to the traditional publication of research in professional, refereed journals: performance texts and electronic publication of texts. Performance texts represent the findings of a study and emphasize sharing and reinterpreting the experiences of the teacher researcher and the researched. These texts can take many forms and are presented as a series of techniques for sharing the actions embedded in the action research. Electronic publication of action research texts offers another means for sharing action research with other classroom teachers and colleagues.

The following criteria for judging action research reports are discussed: intractability of reform, audience, format, prejudices, professional disposition, reflective stance, action taken, the relationship be-tween action and data, the ongoing monitoring of practice, suggested changes, and the responses of colleagues to the action research effort.

Finally, teacher researchers are encouraged to celebrate their actions and to commit to action research as just the beginning of their lifelong learning.

———

After reading this chapter you should be able to

1. Identify strategies to use for sharing your action research inquiry.
2. Identify criteria for judging the quality of action research.
3. Discuss how to celebrate your professional learning and contributions to the field.

Reflecting on Reflective Teaching
MARY-CURTIS GRAMLEY

This is the story of a university professor who worked as the staff development coordinator for an urban elementary school. It provides us with the perspective of someone who worked in a long-term, consultant/facilitator role for fifteen elementary teachers concerned with implementing an action research/reflective practitioner approach in their classrooms. It also illustrates the importance of collaboration in action research at every step of the process—from planning the inquiry to sharing, critiquing, and celebrating the results!

During the 1996–97 school year, teachers and specialists in an elementary school of approximately 310 students in kindergarten through fifth grade moved somewhat reluctantly into the world of action research. This first attempt to implement schoolwide action research projects provided many discoveries about ourselves as learners, researchers, and inquirers. Additionally, the experiences highlighted the value of collaboration in planning and conducting action research projects and in presenting the outcomes of the projects. Several vignettes from our experiences illustrate the value of collaboration in action research.

As a member of the school leadership team responsible for staff development, I helped guide the process of designing and carrying out the projects. One of the major challenges in conducting

action research projects for this particular group of teachers was the first step: defining the question or problem to be studied. The delicate part of the facilitator's role for this part of action research is to guide teachers toward questions that accurately represent their real concerns and to help them articulate questions in ways that clarify the important elements. If action research is to be useful and engaging, then questions must focus on significant issues related to the success of students within the classroom.

While defining a concern and developing a question, one teacher began with some very general thoughts about gender imbalance in her classroom. She had sensed the impact of class composition, that is, fourteen females and seven males, on the interactions among the young students and on the climate within the classroom. The issues, however, were not well formulated and were difficult to translate into specific questions. "Something is going on here," she noted. "But I am not sure what, and I don't know how to turn what I am sensing into a question." Furthermore, it was difficult to determine if there really was a problem and whether it was adversely effecting student success. Although undefined at the outset, this issue seemed to intrigue and puzzle the teacher, so we began to explore some of the specific behaviors the children were demonstrating. As we discussed the teacher's observations, it became clear that a major area of concern was the communication patterns of students and the teacher during large-group discussions and during times when students chose from a variety of independent and cooperative group activities. A question regarding communication patterns emerged from our discussions, and this teacher, who earlier had said she had no idea exactly what question to pursue, launched into her project with enthusiasm and commitment. Collaboration at this beginning stage of the project helped define a question that both motivated and framed the study.

The value of time spent on framing the question was further confirmed by a team of primary teachers who ultimately chose to examine the outcomes of children's participation in activities of their choice. A first- and a second-grade teacher in adjoining classrooms had collaborated in designing independent learning activities (ILA) for the students when they arrived in the morning. While the students appeared to thoroughly enjoy these types of activities, it was not clear whether the experiences were contributing to authentic learning. Additionally, the teachers were concerned about the types of activities certain children consistently chose.

Like the teacher whose classroom presented undefined issues related to gender, these teachers had a series of ambiguous concerns that were difficult to reduce to a single, researchable question. In trying to help them clarify the question that would guide their project, I engaged in a series of observations during independent learning activity time. These observations and the discussions with the teachers regarding student choices and student participation helped clarify the major concern: "Were activities chosen during independent learning time truly valuable, and if so, what was their value?" Although this was a broad concern, we chose to analyze the issues pertaining to independent learning activities in relation to a curriculum framework adopted by the school. The curriculum framework served as a reference point and provided the structure within

which the question would ultimately be framed: "What are the elements of independent learning activities that promote intellectual engagement and depth of knowledge?"

In this case, as in the previous one, the time spent discussing the issues with the teachers both helped them to develop a question and to analyze the issues more deeply. This type of dialogue can involve a group of teachers considering similar problems or individual teachers. Discussion at this initial stage of the process is extremely useful, especially for teachers for who have had little or no experience with action research.

Although discussions at the end of the projects differed significantly from those at the beginning, all members of the school teaching staff benefited from sharing research discoveries at an all-staff celebration that took place at the end of the year. At the celebration, each teacher or team of teachers presented their projects and described the major discoveries. The teacher who focused on gender issues was both open and candid about her discoveries, acknowledging that at first it had been difficult to accept that she was ignoring the persistent requests for attention from one female student. Additionally, the fact that she was calling on two students to a much larger degree than any others in the class was an alarming yet important discovery. This teacher's willingness to share a part of her teaching that she wished to improve encouraged other teachers to look more honestly at their findings and become constructively critical of their own teaching.

At the year-end celebration, the teachers who had examined student participation in independent learning activities made a very interesting presentation in which they described the work of several children over a three-month period. The children's work was then compared with the curriculum framework that had provided some definition for the projects. Teachers were able to see relationships of learning experiences to curriculum design, which was exceedingly helpful as the teachers worked to implement the framework. This project actually initiated analyses of independent learning experiences in several other classrooms.

Although all of the teachers finished the year with a favorable attitude toward action research, all did not begin with this mindset. Research to some of the teachers meant an irrelevant, sometimes contrived activity that usually generated findings of little value and certainly was not worth the effort or the distraction from the "real work of teaching." The interactions and discussions at the beginning of the project and the presentations and conversations at the end were like bookends to support and enclose very productive and positive experiences. Without exception, all of the teachers were looking forward to continuing their professional development by conducting action research projects.

⸭

IT IS UNLIKELY THAT by the time you have arrived at this point in the book you will have actually been through the full action research cycle and are ready to immerse yourself in the next cycle. It is likely, however, that you are currently engaged in the process, perhaps collecting data, undertaking early analysis, monitoring the appropriateness of your data collection, and so on. As the title suggests, this chapter is about examining and celebrating the insights gained through action research. And although it may be premature, given the stage you are at in the process, to discuss its critical evaluation and "public debut," it is appropriate to consider some of those issues now.

Sharing Action Research

One way that teacher researchers can gain additional insight and satisfaction from their action research is to share their work with other members of the teaching profession. The act of sharing and celebrating the findings of action research is a critical component of the professional disposition of teaching that will ultimately revitalize the culture of teaching and move us from a *craft culture* to a *reflective practitioner* focused profession.

As discussed earlier, the historical gap between research and practice has also been fueled by the resistance of teacher researchers to share or publish their research with a wider community of learners. It is with this obstacle in mind that performance texts and electronic publication are offered as alternatives for presenting teacher research reports as well as for engaging colleagues, and yourself, in the reinterpretation of your findings.

Performance Texts as a Means for Sharing Action Research

The most obvious way to share what you have learned through action research is to discuss the findings of your study with other teachers and administrators in your school. Denzin (1997) has proposed performance texts as one way to share and interpret the findings of a study. In contrast to a static, written document published in a refereed journal, performance texts allow alternative representations of action research work in a way that teacher researchers can reinterpret their work while at the same time engaging colleagues in the lived experiences of those involved in the action research process.

So what exactly is a performance text? According to Denzin (1997), a **performance text** is an interpretive event, a rehearsed or improvised creative set of activities performed to benefit an audience and the performers. Performers use props including manuscripts, lighting, and music for their performances to try to bring their texts alive for the audience. They do this in many ways. They may choose to read their text to an audience, or they may use pictures, slides, photographs, show a film, use audiovisual aides, bring in music, lip sync words set to a musical text, or create a scholarly version of an MTV text. During the performance, audiences are neither pure voyeurs nor passive recipients of performance. For example, the teacher researcher can bring the audience into the performance, do a sing-along, hand out a script, give audience members speaking parts, or make a communal performance out of the text (Denzin, 1997).

The use of performance texts can address what has been a problem with the action research community—the hesitancy or unwillingness of teacher researchers to share their work. Performance texts offer alternatives to traditional technical papers produced for publication that in the past haven't been done or have had little impact on practice. At the risk of oversimplifying Denzin's performance texts concepts, it is worth considering how teacher researchers can embrace performance texts as a powerful strategy for sharing with and engaging colleagues in the action research process as we strive to put action in our work.

One form of action, therefore, is to share your work with colleagues in a persuasive manner and through the performance to gain a greater understanding of and appreciation for the inquiry you have undertaken. Performance texts are effective because they can help both action researchers and their colleagues to share and interpret the action research inquiry, making it meaningful even for those not directly involved in it.

Sharing the Lived Experience

Performance texts can be a powerful technique for sharing with colleagues the lived experience of students and the uneasiness that lead you to the investigation in the first place. For example, your inquiry may have focused on the effect of math manipulatives on student learning, in particular, the multiplication of fractions. After all, we *all* know the rule "Invert and multiply." But how many of us really know *why?* What does the use of manipulatives contribute to the students' understanding of the problem? By having colleagues experience vignettes that characterize the lived experiences of students, you will create the "evocative moment when another's experiences comes alive for the self" (Denzin, 1997, p. 95). For example, engaging colleagues in an activity involving the use of math manipulatives may create frustration and confusion and an awareness of the problems faced by students, and teachers of mathematics, to construct meaningful conceptual and procedural knowledge in mathematics—especially as it applies to the multiplication of fractions.

Interpreting the Lived Experience

So what are the implications of having shared in this lived experience of the students' learning multiplication of fractions? As the rest of the story unfolds through the performance text, both the audience and researchers may offer implications that had not been considered previously. This collaborative, collegial activity can be a catalyst for brainstorming possible implications and build commitment to changing what has happened in the past. For example, if we all knew that the students in our class or school performed poorly on math assessments, particularly in relation to their conceptual knowledge of fractions, sharing in and interpreting that experience may mobilize us to improve how we teach fractions in particular and mathematics in general.

Performance Texts Techniques

Denzin (1997) has recommended an extensive list of techniques for sharing texts compared to just reading accounts to colleagues. After all, how many of us have rolled our eyes at the colleague, principal, or university professor who profess to know something about effective teaching and then proceed to bore us by reading a report (which we have a copy of) to us? And while Denzin's list includes everything from audiovisual aids to an MTV performance, teacher researchers might use performance texts to model what they believe or have learned through their action research efforts to be effective teaching strategies. Not all strategies we use with children (for example, "Let's sit on the mat in a circle") will transfer to adult learners, but many constructivist techniques, in science and mathematics education, for instance, will actively engage the audience in your, and their, learning. Key Concepts Box 7–1 lists performance texts options.

KEY CONCEPTS BOX 7–1

Performance Texts Options
Role-play.
Videotape a classroom activity.
Use drama.
Incorporate music.
Share a reading of text.
Add interactive multimedia.
Show pictures, slides, photographs, or video.
Use other audiovisual aids.

One technique that Denzin does not discuss is the use of interactive multimedia software as a way to share and engage colleagues in the text. I have seen teacher researchers use PowerPoint, Hyperstudio, and Director to great effect by incorporating sound, pictures, and video into presentations. I have witnessed teacher researchers develop their multimedia presentations with active engagement of the audience in mind. Maybe we are not far from performance texts that allow participants to choose their own happy endings (as per some CD-ROM games that my six year old plays with). Ultimately, the experience provides a venue for teacher researchers and colleagues to grapple with the fundamental question of "What is going on here?" related to the teacher researcher's area of focus.

Now is not the time to be self-conscious. Be bold. Attempt more, gain more (and perhaps experience more pain and embarrassment). Take a risk, comforted by the knowledge that you have the potential to motivate colleagues to create meaning from the experience.

Electronic Means for Sharing Action Research

In an era of increasing use of technology to enhance teaching and learning, as evidenced by the influx of computers in schools and the homes of our students, we are constantly exposed to electronic media—the Internet, web sites, on-line shopping for airfare bargains, and of course, professional literature databases such as ERIC! However, a public forum such as the Internet also provides for freedom of speech in ways that are not always socially acceptable, for example, web sites that highlight violence, child pornography, and so on. In short, anyone with the computer hardware, software, and necessary computer literacy skills can create a web site on the Internet.

My assumption, however, is that most of us do not have all of the hardware, software, skills, and time (!) to develop a web site. Furthermore, if we ignore the existing action research web sites being used for sharing action research, we are limiting our conversation to teacher researchers who go exploring the Internet in search of new action research web sites (see chapter 8 for a complete discussion of on-line action research resources).

Perhaps one of the most exciting web sites for electronic sharing of teacher research is *Networks: An On-Line Journal for Teacher Research* (http://www.oise. utoronto.ca/~ctd/networks/). Teacher researchers wishing to share their investigations, either completed or in progress, can submit a contribution to one of the following four sections of this on-line journal:

- Full-length articles (2,000–3,000 words) reporting a completed action research inquiry.
- Shorter articles (300–750 words) describing a work in progress or raising issues related to such work.
- Book reviews (750–1,000 words).
- A calendar of teacher researcher events providing teacher researchers with information about upcoming action research events.

Contributions to be considered for publication in *Networks* can be submitted in any of the following forms:

- Email message to networks-j@oise.utoronto.ca.
- A personal web page address (URL) at which the text may be read.
- Hard copy of manuscript, with or without accompanying disk (*Networks* Homepage).

Electronic sharing allows teacher researchers to share their work and engage in conversation with professionals from around the world who are investigating similar problems. It is an opportunity for us to learn from each other and to contribute to the existing knowledge base—something that teacher researchers have not done historically.

Publishing in an on-line teacher researcher journal like *Networks* is different from publishing in a traditional, refereed (hard copy) journal and has different purposes:

> The purpose of placing action research accounts on the Web is to make them part of the conversations/correspondences between action researchers in which individuals and groups are helping each other to take their learning and inquiries forward. (Jack Whitehead, personal email, 1998)

In this sense, the sharing of teacher researchers' accounts is not seen as the end of the action research process, but as a part of the process—an opportunity to discuss our research with interested teacher researchers.

Networks also provide an opportunity for teacher researchers to have their work "refereed" by a panel of three reviewers, of whom at least two are practicing teacher researchers (members of the editorial board), and critiqued using criteria that include the following:

- Address an issue of significance to other teachers and teacher researchers;
- Provide information about the methods of data collection and analysis of evidence that will be useful to other teacher researchers;
- Provide adequate information about the institutional/educational context, bearing in mind an international readership;
- Present a clear and coherent account, with appropriate warrant for the conclusions reached;
- Comment on the implications and issues arising from the research in a way that can potentially contribute to an ongoing debate;
- Appropriately take account of and acknowledge the work of other writers;
- Be written in an interesting, reader-friendly style. (*Networks* Homepage)

If teacher researchers begin to accept publishing of action research as an important part of their professional disposition, on-line journals such as *Networks* will go a long way toward providing an accessible, appropriate forum for teachers to present and celebrate their learnings. As the editor of *Networks* points out:

For practitioners' inquiries to achieve their full potential, however, it is essential that they be widely disseminated. Not only are good ideas worth sharing, whether they be suggestions for practice arising from the research or insights gained through reflection on the significance of what was discovered in the light of wider reading; but equally the description of the decisions made and routes taken in carrying out these inquiries can be helpful to other teacher researchers who are still planning their own inquiries. . . . A further reason for starting this journal is to increase awareness of the widespread interest and involvement in classroom inquiry and to facilitate contact between individuals and groups who might not otherwise know of each other's existence. Our hope is that, through this opportunity to communicate with a wider audience, teacher researchers will more fully perceive their work as participating in, and contributing to, a larger knowledge building community. (*Networks* Homepage)

For an example of the kinds of research being published on-line at *Networks,* go to the homepage and check out the "Journal" table of contents (see Figure 7-1 for a screen capture from *Networks* journal).

A Word on Quality Control on the Web

The electronic sharing of action research reports has not been without its challenges. Issues of quality and what should be placed in the public domain of the Internet are common concerns for all teachers and parents. Nevertheless, the potential of the Internet to provide a global forum for professionals should not be underestimated. The issue of quality becomes a professional and personal responsibility for those of us who choose to "post" information and opinions on the Web. Associated with quality is the issue of control, that is quality control. Who should be responsible for controlling the quality of action research posted on the Web?

But Is It Really Research? Criteria for Judging Action Research

As you should be aware of by now, action research is different from traditional educational research in many ways. By definition, it is research done *by* and *for* teachers and students, not research done *on* them. As such, the methods for *doing* action research and the methods for *sharing* action research are uniquely suited to its special purposes. Given these distinctions, what are the criteria for *evaluating* action research? Should these criteria be the same as those applied to educational research published in refereed journals?

Jack Whitehead doesn't think so, on the basis that the findings of action research are usually formatted differently from the findings of traditional educational research. He maintains, "The spiritual, aesthetic and ethical standards of judgment in educational action research require multi-media forms of presentation which cannot, by their nature, be communicated through the pages of the linguistically constrained refereed journals" (Jack Whitehead, personal email, 1998).

Ian Hughes, editor of the *Action Research Electronic Reader,* says that when making publication decisions, he "does not try for the standard which I imagine is

 **An On-line Journal for Teacher Research**

 **Home**

Welcome to NETWORKS: AN ON-LINE JOURNAL FOR TEACHER RESEARCH. This is the first on-line journal dedicated to teacher research.

With the help of readers and writers like you, this journal will soon provide a forum for teachers' voices, a place where teachers working in classrooms, from pre-school to university, can share their experiences and learn from each other. We have created this "sample" web site as an introduction to what we hope will become a valuable contribution to educational research.

Throughout this web site, you will find feature-length articles, as well as short reports of work-in-progress, book reviews, and discussions on current issues in teacher research. Topics will cover a wide variety of issues related to classroom research including: curriculum, methodology, ethics, collaboration, and community.

For more information on becoming a contributor to NETWORKS, please review our notes for contributors. We also plan to develop a comprehensive list of web sites relevant to teacher research and to provide updated information on action research events. The forthcoming "Discussion Forum" site will serve as an interactive centre of communication between authors and readers.

Join us as we embark on this exciting new venture! Share your classroom research with colleagues from around the world.

Thank you for visiting the NETWORKS web site.

Journal

Discussion Forum	Research News

Navigation Tips	Notes for Contributors

FIGURE 7-1 *Networks* Journal Screen Capture

appropriate to a peer-reviewed journal" and does not set "a standard which is impossibly high" because he is "not trying to compete with established academic journals." He believes that "the purpose and uses of my electronic reader are different." Because of this unique purpose, these are the informal criteria he uses when evaluating electronic action research texts for on-line publication:

- Would (in my imperfect judgment) the proposed paper be of potential use to this audience?
- Is the intended audience graduate students and practitioners of action research in fields including (but not limited to) health and community development?
- Does the article generally conform to accepted standards for publication in the social sciences, with references properly cited (in a format consistent within each article)?
- Does the paper contain original research or analysis (rather than being a re-hash of an existing publication)? Is there any hint of plagiarism?
- Is the article short, and written (if possible) in a simple and direct style? (Ian Hughes, personal email, 1998)

Others offer additional advice about criteria for judging action research reports. Tickle (1993) recommends you assess the quality of your action research work and the work of others on the basis of the following characteristics:

- **Prudence**—practical wisdom and the capacity to judge the most profitable courses of action.
- **Openness**—records, representation of action, reports of underlying theories, reviews of evidence of these, responsiveness to reviews, reinterpretations of accounts.
- **Communal Self-Reflection**—exposure of prejudices, both as practitioner and as researcher; engaging in collective examination of prejudices.
- **Courage**—in exposing curriculum proposals and practice; and in exposing research endeavours.
- **Growth**—a willingness to change and acknowledge change.
- **Contemplation**—living with the fermentation of understanding, especially of the theory-practice relationship, while seeking maturation.
- **Overview**—appreciating the interdependence of phenomena.
- **Configuration**—making meaningful form from complex information. (Tickle, 1993, p. 235)

Another way to judge the quality of action research is to compare the written account of the process and findings to the characteristics of action research discussed in chapter 1: Is it participatory and democratic? Does the knowledge gained from action research liberate students and teachers? Do teacher researchers have decision-making authority? Are teacher researchers committed to continued professional development and school improvement?

Tickle (1993) has argued that focusing too much energy on developing criteria for judging action research can have the unanticipated outcome of "freezing" would-be action researchers. These criteria, however, can help you judge the quality of your own work and decide how to improve the quality of your action research effort. Each of us who accept the responsibility of being a self-governing professional must apply some or all of the criteria listed for judging the quality of the action research accounts that we read or experience in some other forum.

Based on a number of evaluative schema, including those listed above, I have devised the simple list of questions shown in Research in Action Checklist 7-1 to help you assess and evaluate your own action research efforts and the efforts of others:

RESEARCH IN ACTION CHECKLIST 7-1

Criteria for Judging Action Research

_____ **Intractability of Reform**—Does your action research lead to an action?

_____ **Audience**—What is the intended audience for your report?

_____ **Format**—Have you presented the report using an acceptable format?

_____ **Prejudices**—Have you shared any prejudices that may have affected your findings?

_____ **Professional Disposition**—How has the action research effort contributed to your professional disposition?

_____ **Reflective Stance**—In what ways has the action research effort contributed to your reflective stance on the way you view teaching and learning?

_____ **Life-Enhancing**—How have your efforts enhanced the lives of the students in your care?

_____ **Action**—What action have you taken?

_____ **Action-Data Connection**—How is the proposed action connected to your data analysis and interpretation?

_____ **Impact**—How will you monitor the effects of your practice?

_____ **Changes**—What would you do differently next time?

_____ **Colleague Response**—How did your colleagues respond to your findings and the actions recommended by your research?

Celebration—It's Time to Party!

For decades education and the profession of teaching have been the whipping post for all that ails society. As Deal (1987) has argued:

> In the field of education, two decades of criticism, desegregation, innovation, and frustration have eroded faith and confidence in schools. . . . During these decades, schools were asked to solve the problems of the society, but to make their solutions inexpensive. Schools have been soundly criticized for not accomplishing feats that lie outside the ability of the society to perform. These have been turbulent times for educators, and there is no reason to believe that the turbulence will subside in the near future. (p. 9)

Like Deal, I am not overly optimistic that the turbulent times that teachers endured are all in the past. We continue to face tremendous obstacles: the national deficit, the spread of AIDS, the increase in teen pregnancy, the increase in racial tension, and the poor performance of our children on international tests, just to name a few (c.f. the results of the TIMSS study, U.S. National Research Center, 1996). In a nutshell, if it's not one thing it's another, and those of us in the teaching profession are often blamed.

While these assertions may not be warranted, over time, these claims and others like them have eroded the self-esteem and sense of self-efficacy of teachers. And while being a teacher researcher is not the only solution, it *can* contribute to rebuilding our individual and collective self-esteem and sense of self-efficacy, because it provides an opportunity for us to celebrate, as a learning community, what we have learned as teacher researchers and how these learnings will positively affect the lives of children. In Deal's words, it is an opportunity to rebuild the "faith and confidence" that our constituents have in schools.

Teacher researchers can evoke faith and confidence in themselves and their schools by sharing their findings with the school community in ways that reinforce the importance of professional, systematic inquiry into one's practice and the resulting impact it has on children in schools. One way for this to happen is through a *celebration* of teacher researchers' learnings that may be supported by staff development funding, PTO/PTA contributions, or any other appropriate source of funding that can be located. Alternatively, teachers and other interested members of the school community can participate in a potluck dinner or perhaps coordinate the celebration with a state or national teachers' day of recognition that again provides a forum for teacher researchers to celebrate their action research achievements.

As Stringer has noted:

> Celebration is an important part of community-based work. It not only satisfies the very human, emotional elements of the experience, it works to enhance participants' feelings of solidarity, competence, and general well-being. It is a time when the emotional energy expended in particularly difficult activity can be recharged, and when any residual antagonisms developed during the project can be defused and relationships among stakeholders enhanced. (1996, p. 140)

A celebration can take many forms. Over the years, we have celebrated action research courses with poster sessions in which teacher researchers have informally shared their work using a performance of their choosing while incorporating food, drink, and music to accentuate the festive nature of the celebration.

There is no foolproof recipe for a successful party. We have all attended parties that have made us yearn to be somewhere else—even sitting in a dentist's chair has appeared more attractive! Rather than trying to suggest a recipe for a successful celebration, let's keep it simple: If you and your colleagues are excited about your learnings and express interest in "getting together" to celebrate your action research efforts, go for it. It is a great opportunity to recharge your batteries and to recommit to the process that will follow in the next action research cycle. If, on the other hand, this process has only reinforced your belief that your colleagues have nothing left to contribute to the profession, it may be more prudent to thank them for their contribution and make a dental appointment for a six-month cleaning (and hope that there is no need for a root canal)!

This Is Just the Beginning!

It should come as no surprise that I suggest toward the end of this book that *now* is really the beginning of your work. At this point, you have invested considerable time and energy reading about action research, learning how to do action research, locating action research within the broader framework of socially responsive research, and developing your own action research efforts; clarifying an area of focus, establishing data collection techniques, undertaking data analysis and interpretation, and formulating an action plan through the use of a Steps to Action Chart. In short, you have done much work in a relatively short amount of time.

But now comes the real test of any educational innovation. Can it become a critical component of your regular, ongoing teaching practice? If you have found ways to overcome the potential obstacles to incorporating action research into the reflective practice stance you now have, you are well on your way to living the life of a reflective teacher researcher. Living this professional life, in the ways it has been described here, has the potential to change the culture of schools so that as a professional community we can once again evoke the faith and confidence of our communities in our schools and our profession of teaching.

We can all think of reasons why we shouldn't be incorporating action research into our craft culture—most notably because we are challenged by the impediments of time and resources. However, if you believe in what you are doing, you will find a way to make it happen. Call me an idealist if you will, but I am constantly impressed by the positive nature of teachers who, faced with adversity and challenges, are able to find ways to make a positive difference in children's lives. Make no mistake, that is what this action research journey has been about.

Armed with your knowledge, skills, values, and attitudes about action research, the work now begins as you routinize the practice and continue to monitor the effects of your innovations on students' learning, openly accepting the credo for professional practice and living the life of a lifelong learner. What you are learning about your practice will ultimately enhance the lives of the children in your care.

Summary

The chapter explained ways for sharing, evaluating, and celebrating action research. Performance texts are ways to represent and reinterpret the findings of an action research study by sharing the lived experiences of the researcher and the researched. Publication of action research stories in an electronic medium also provides a means for sharing action research with others. These techniques are viable alternatives to the traditional "papers" or journal articles that are rarely written, or shared, by teacher researchers.

The criteria for judging the quality of action research include questions about the intractability of reform, audience, format, prejudices, professional disposition, reflective stance, action taken, the relationship between action and data, the ongoing monitoring of practice, suggested changes, and the responses of colleagues to the action research effort.

Finally, the chapter discusses the need for teachers to celebrate their learnings while also committing to action research as a regular component of their professional disposition—for this is just the beginning—not the end of our journey as lifelong learners.

For Further Thought

1. What alternative techniques could you adapt to share the findings of your action research efforts?
2. How does your action research report satisfy the criteria for judging action research?
3. What plans do you have for celebrating your learnings? (Please send me a virtual invitation!)
4. What will the next spiral of your teacher researcher life look like?
5. What would you need to do to submit your action research report for publication to *Networks*?

CHAPTER 8

On-Line Action
Research Resources

This chapter provides an overview of the on-line resources available to teacher researchers. These resources provide an important support network for like-minded teachers all over the world who use the Internet to share ideas and communicate the findings of their work. The sites discussed in this chapter will be especially helpful for teacher researchers who feel somewhat isolated in their efforts to conduct research and who welcome an audience and feedback.

On-line resources for action research fall into the following categories:

- *Action Research Web Sites Sponsored by Universities*—These sites provide links to discussions, calendars of events, other sites of interest, on-line action research courses, and so on.
- *Listservs that Provide Opportunities to Discuss Critical Issues*—Leaders in the field of action research participate in on-line discussions and often provide feedback to neophyte teacher researchers seeking assistance.
- *On-line Action Research Journals and Other Related Literature*—For example, *Networks*, tables of contents, abstracts, and links to full-text articles available on-line.

After reading this chapter you should be able to

1. Locate on-line action research resources such as web sites, listservs, and journals.
2. Participate in on-line action research conversations by subscribing to a listserv.

■■

Teaching and Learning on the Web—A Personal Reflection
GEOFF MILLS

Geoff Mills, the author of this textbook, is a professor at Southern Oregon University. This vignette describes his experiences and the challenges he faced when he was asked by his university's distance learning division to teach an action research class via EdNet, Internet, and live instruction. His own action research project, modeled for his class as the semester unfolded, asked the two-pronged question: "What are the effects of this multimedia approach on student achievement and attitude?"

A number of Oregon universities use an interactive video system (EdNet) that provides distance learning opportunities for teachers who wish to take classes for credit but are unable (or unwilling) to drive to the university to participate in a traditional face-to-face contact class. My university is a regional institution that provides service to students throughout the southern half of the state, thus giving access to students who may live over 100 miles from the university.

While these distance learning classes are taken in "real time," university students are able to attend a downlink site (such as the local community's hospital, school district office, community college, and so on) that has satellite communication capabilities. Students receive the class via an audio and video link but also have the capability (and expectation) to be interactive. Students are able to communicate with the instructor through electronic hand waving that signals the student's intent to ask a question or make a comment. Simultaneously, there is a "live" group of students at the origin site who must also learn to use the "push-to-talk" button system. That is, for them to

be heard and seen by their classmates in remote areas, they must essentially push a microphone button that also signals to the technician in the control booth that there is someone other than the instructor talking and hence the camera can be moved to focus on the student who is speaking. The same is true at the remote sites, where technicians are also present to direct the cameras and attend to any technical difficulties, as well as to administer exams, conduct course evaluations, and so on.

To decrease the expensive use of satellite time, I was asked to adapt my action research class to a format that incorporated contact time via the course's homepage on the Internet as well as the use of a listserv. Thus the adventure of using on-line resources commenced. I'm not sure that I'm quite ready to completely give up face-to-face contact with students to increase access, although the changing landscape of distance learning suggests otherwise.

I must confess that this was anything but a smooth transition as I struggled with how to make the course engaging and interactive via the virtual university medium. I was constantly bombarded with email from students who were also struggling with the challenges presented by the technology we were being encouraged (forced?) to use. With fifty students in the course (of whom only fifteen were "live"), I struggled to learn names and the faces attached to them. In my estimation, the rapport and interpersonal relationships that I hold as sacred with my students suffered considerably. Nevertheless, we continued to work with the instructional system that had been forced upon us and to learn from our mistakes as we went along.

I should note, however, that teaching via EdNet and the Internet provided a particular challenge given that there were teachers enrolled in the course who not only did not want to use the technology ("I don't even use an automatic teller machine. Why would I want to use a computer?!"), but vehemently opposed the use of the technology on the basis of "Who will be watching our communication?" A certain kind of technophobia seemed to be present and challenged the viability of the course. We struggled to make the on-line interactions engaging and something other than a venue for people to vent. Compounding the issues related to the on-line component of the course were ongoing problems with the (up until then reliable) satellite links, which forced me to send videotapes of the class sessions to participants.

During this class, I took the opportunity to model for my students action research on my own teaching along the lines of, "What were the effects of this multimedia approach on student achievement and attitude?" In the end, my action research findings into the effects of this innovation on student achievement and attitude were insightful, if not surprising. Participants in the class produced many fine action research projects that they presented at a live "celebration" during the final week of the class. Apparently student achievement had not suffered due to the use of the multimedia presentation of course material.

However, the news on student attitude was not as pleasing. Many students had been frustrated to the point of dropping the class because of the need to use computer communication. Some claimed that had there been a choice (in my mind there *had* been a choice—take the course at another time) they would have dropped the course and taken it when they knew there would be more contact with the instructor—even if it was satellite-mediated contact. The message for me was clear: University students still wanted real contact with the teacher. However, students who had persevered with the communication and resources on the Internet had a very positive feeling about the experience. Students felt that they were pioneers in the venture (in 1995), and many thrived in the environment. All in all—a mixed bag. We are more technologically sophisticated now than we were then and can now more fully take advantage of the learning opportunities provided by the Internet.

■■

ON-LINE ACTION research resources provide a wonderful forum for teacher researchers to reach out and discuss significant issues with like-minded teacher researchers, university-based action researchers, and practitioners from other disciplines (such as nursing, environmental education, and sociology) who are applying action research to address their own field-based problems. Internet resources offered by groups all over the world provide a truly international learning community in which conversations and requests for assistance can be undertaken in a safe environment. Between the listservs (on-line discussion groups), web sites, and literature related to action research there is something for everyone. As one search engine command proclaims, "Go get it."

Using the Internet to Get Connected

My experiences of teaching in an Australian primary school (K–7) and teaching at universities in Australia and the United States (and watching my six-year-old son in kindergarten) is that teaching shares many of the characteristics of kindergarten and preschool play—as teachers we tend to work in isolation, engaged in parallel play in our own little sandboxes. It has been argued that one of the critical contributing factors to teacher burnout is the isolated nature of the profession. Clearly, many teachers find little solace in the isolation of their workplace. One of the characteristics of action research is that it is "collaborative" or "participatory." And while we hope that teacher researchers are able to engage in this systematic inquiry as a learning community, there is the distinct possibility that you will find yourself working alone on some aspect of the action research process. Regardless of the degree to which you participate in this activity with others, the ability to interact with other practitioners via the Internet can provide a valuable support system, a way to become "connected" to others with similar goals and interests.

Access to web-based action research resources can provide teacher researchers with the sense that the world is smaller and can be easily reached from their home, school, or office computer. I was reminded of the shrinking nature of the world during a trip to Australia to visit my eighty-four-year-old father, who appeared smaller and weaker than I had remembered him. Not only has the world shrunk over time, but so have some of the artifacts that I use as reference points— such as my dad. Each time I see him (usually every one to two years), he greets with me with the same whimsical smile and turn of phrase, "Where did you come from?!" It's not that he doesn't remember who I am or where I live, but his reference point is a different era than mine, a time of steamship travel to fight in a war half way around the world—two experiences I will never have. So, it was a surprise to him when I talked about being able to write to him on email (electronic mail as compared to "snail" mail) via his assisted living facility's computer, or even directly to him via a fax located in the facility's main office. These were not easy concepts for him to grasp—even if he wanted to.

For those of us who find ourselves in our own little sandbox isolated from likeminded colleagues who do not offer to play with us, the Internet provides an excellent opportunity to participate in an ongoing dialogue with other teacher researchers.

What Different Types of On-Line Resources Can I Use?

The on-line resources offered at different sites typically fall into three categories: action research web sites, listservs, and on-line journals.

Action Research Web Sites

Many action research web sites offer similar features and "links" to other sites of interest. We will briefly review four of these: PARnet (Participatory Action Research Network) based at Cornell University (USA), CARN (Collaborative Action Research Network) based at the University of East Anglia (UK), CARPP (Centre for Action Research in Professional Practice), and Geoff Mills' action research web site.

Participatory Action Research Network (PARnet)

The welcome page to PARnet (http://parnet.org) provides the following context to the site:

Based at Cornell University in the beautiful Finger Lakes region of central New York State, PARnet serves an international group of students, faculty, and other practitioners who share a commitment to promoting high standards of intellectual and social integrity in doing social research for social change. . . . We hope you enjoy the PARnet web site and will take time to share your knowledge and experiences with others. (Participatory Action Research Network, http://parnet.org)

Once you have entered PARnet you are provided with the following choices:

- Events at Cornell.
- Events Worldwide.
- "Parchives."
- Electronic Forums.
- Other Web Sites.
- Where to Study.
- Find Colleagues.
- Consultants.
- *Action Research International* (a refereed on-line journal).

Each of these headings provides you with links to areas such as the archives of the Arlist listserv, a calendar of events (including upcoming conferences), course offerings at Cornell University, the PARtalk listserv (with an invitation to subscribe and with links to other listservs, archives, and information), a link to on-line action research publications, a registry for locating action research colleagues, and finally a toolbox of frequently asked questions (FAQs) about PARnet and how best to use the system. There is plenty here to occupy your time, but it is worth checking out a number of sites before deciding whether to subscribe to any given listserv or journal or to enroll in an action research course.

The Collaborative Action Research Network (CARN)

The Collaborative Action Research Network (www.uea.ac.uk/care/carn) is based at the University of East Anglia (UK) in the Centre for Applied Research in Education (CARE). Unlike most other action research web sites, CARN limits access to their discussion list until a membership is paid. However, other resources that are part of the CARN offerings can be accessed without the fee, for example, the CARN mission statement, links to publications, conference information, and links to other web sites.

Like PARnet, CARN is a wonderful resource for teacher researchers who wish to learn from and contribute to discussions about their action research efforts.

Centre for Action Research in Professional Practice (CARPP)

The Centre for Action Research in Professional Practice (www.bath.ac.uk/carpp) is housed at the University of Bath (UK). The Centre aims to provide support for teacher researchers who are developing their reflective practice. The web site also provides links to graduate action research courses and degree programs at the University of Bath, upcoming conferences, full-text papers (written by Centre staff), and other on-line publications, including unpublished masters and doctoral theses.

Geoff Mills' Action Research Web Site

Another useful resource you may want to explore is the action research web site I have developed in conjunction with my own action research classes and the Oregon Public Education Network (OPEN): (http://beta.open.k12.or.us/arowhelp). This web site includes links to AskERIC, links to other action research web sites, directions for how to subscribe to Arlist, links to on-line journals, instructions for how to register for an on-line action research course, and a clearinghouse of action research investigations conducted by teachers in Oregon.

Listservs

A **listserv** is an on-line discussion forum usually "hosted" by a university computer network. Different groups offer different listservs that are invitations to participate in discussions with other action researchers from all over the world. The most heavily subscribed action research listserv is **Arlist**, which can be subscribed to by following the directions provided by the Arlist homepage:

> To join Arlist you need to send an email message to *listproc@scu.edu.au* with nothing in the subject line, and this message only:
>> subscribe arlist name1 name2
>
> Of course, put your names instead of 'name1 name2'. Remember, this email must go with your own email address. . . . When you subscribe you will get instructions on how to use arlist. (http://elmo.scu.edu.au/schools/sawd/ari/arlist.html)

A word of caution for new listserv users: If you subscribe to a listserv, be prepared to receive a reasonable volume of email messages (maybe five to ten) a day. If you don't check your email every day, this quickly adds up to a great deal of mail. Yet, participation in such an activity appears to be worth the effort. In the time that I have been a subscriber, I have "lurked" (read the messages only, and not actively participated in discussions) on the listserv and been impressed with the thoughtfulness of the discourse as well as the willingness of participants to suggest particular references that may be helpful. Similarly, the advice given to teacher researchers on how best to tackle a problem, what data collection techniques are most appropriate, how to proceed with data analysis and interpretation, and so on have been of high quality. For all of these reasons it is worthwhile for teacher researchers to subscribe to this free resource.

On-Line Journals

Increasingly, full-text, refereed, on-line teacher researcher journals are becoming available. Four such journals are *Educational Action Research*, *Networks*, *Action Research International*, and *the Action Research Electronic Reader*.

Educational Action Research

This journal can be accessed through the CARN homepage or directly at http://www.triangle.co.uk/ear-o.htm. The welcome screen provides some helpful information about the journal as well as subscription directions:

Educational Action Research is a fully refereed international journal concerned with exploring the unity between educational research and practice. Increasing interest in action research in recent years has been accompanied by the development of a number of different approaches: for example, to promote reflective practice; professional development; empowerment; understanding of tacit professional knowledge; curriculum development; institutional change; and development of democratic management and administration. Proponents of all these share the common aim of ending the dislocation of research from practice, an aim which links them with those involved in participatory research and action inquiry. (http://www.triangle.co.uk/ear-o.htm)

By clicking on the "Recent Contents" button, you can quickly access the journal's table of contents and some the articles for which full text is available. Each author is linked to an abstract of his or her paper and, if available, a link is provided to an on-line copy. In many cases the authors' email addresses are also provided so readers can communicate directly with them. This is particularly helpful to teacher researchers wishing to break down isolation and to seek feedback on their school-based action research efforts.

By providing the *Educational Action Research* table of contents on-line, the publisher has made a valuable contribution to bridging the gap between research and practice by addressing one of the potential obstacles hypothesized by Mary Kennedy (1997), that is, the accessibility of research for teachers. By reviewing what is available on-line from a teacher-friendly journal, teacher researchers can access a journal article and even initiate a conversation with the author. This is a valuable way of seeking clarification about the content of published articles, as well as an opportunity to gain advice from authors who are very willing to help. For some of us reflecting back on the "good old days" when immersing oneself in the literature meant foraging through card catalogues and "the stacks," this virtual library and interaction with authors signals a giant step in the right direction.

Networks

An on-line journal for teacher research (http://www.oise.utoronto.ca/~ctd/networks/), *Networks* is the first on-line journal dedicated to teacher research that has full-length articles available (see chapter 7). This exciting journal has the potential to make a considerable contribution to the literature on action research by providing a forum for teachers to publish their action research accounts on-line.

The journal homepage also provides links to a "discussion forum" listserv, "notes for contributors," "navigation tips," and "research news." As the homepage proclaims, this journal is an invitation to "share your classroom research with colleagues from around the world."

Action Research International

This journal can be accessed through the PARnet homepage or at http://www.scu.edu.au/schools/sawd/ari/ari-home.html. According to the journal's homepage:

Action Research International is a refereed on-line journal of action research. It has a distinguished international advisory panel, and is sponsored by the Institute

Key On-Line Addresses	
PARNet	http://parnet.org
CARN	http://www.uea.ac.uk/care/carn
CARPP	http://www.bath.ac.uk/carpp/
Geoff Mills' website	http://open.k12.or.us/arowhelp/
Arlist	http://elmo.scu.edu.au/schools/sawd/ari/arlist.html or email: listproc@scu.edu.au
Action Research Electronic Reader	http://www.beh.cchs.usyd.edu.au/~arow/Reader/welcome.htm
Educational Action Research	http://www.triangle.co.uk/ear-o.htm
Networks	http://www.oise.utoronto.ca/~ctd/networks/
Action Research International	http://www.scu.edu.au/schools/sawd/ari/ari-home.html
AROWHelp	http://open.k12.or.us/arowhelp/

of Workplace Research Learning and Development (WoRLD) within the School of Social and Workplace Development (SaWD) and by Southern Cross University Press. (http://www.scu.edu.au/schools/sawd/ari/ari-home.html)

The journal also provides links to other web sites and directions for how to subscribe to the journal and submit papers.

Action Research Electronic Reader

This journal can be accessed at http://www.beh.cchs.usyd.edu.au/~arow/Reader/welcome.htm. Like the other journals, the *Action Research Electronic Reader* posts links to current and past refereed journal articles that can be downloaded to your computer. It also provides another venue for teacher researchers to publish their own stories. (See Key Concepts Box 8-1 for a list of on-line addresses.)

On-Line Action Research: Challenges and Cautions

While the use of the Internet may be convenient for some of us and perhaps even preferred over face-to-face contact (like using an automatic teller machine!), you should be aware of a few challenges and cautions.

The Challenge of Technophobia

The Internet can literally provide a "web" of connections and resources for you as a teaching professional. However, this wonderful resource cannot be accessed if you suffer from **technophobia**, or fear of things mechanical, electrical, or digital. This chapter is based on the assumption that you are willing and able to accept the challenge provided by the Web and to profit from the interactions such a medium offers. Increasingly, graduates from teacher preparation programs (and high school for that matter) are required to demonstrate computer literacy skills. And while many of us remember an era sans automatic teller machines, computer chip cars, and regular flights to outer space, grappling our way into the twenty-first century technology base is, to paraphrase Apollo astronaut Neil Armstrong, "A giant step for humankind!"

Many of us face frustrations around the relatively simple act of turning on ("booting up") a computer. No doubt we all know adults (you might be one of them!) who are intimidated by computer technology and would have considerable difficulty completing such basic tasks even if they wanted to. As the chapter-opening vignette illustrates, I too was dragged into the era of satellite communication, technology-enhanced curriculum, and automatic teller machines! Give yourself the time to make mistakes and be prepared to learn how to use the technology from the students in your class, for this is their generation and many of them have skills far exceeding our own. For example, my six-year-old son has no difficulty turning on our home computer and inserting his CD-ROM game of choice (seems like "Quest for Camelot" is the flavor of the month). He is able to navigate through the games on the CD and demonstrates reading skills by being able to identify the correct buttons to click on. Using the mouse, he is also able to shut down the computer when he is finished playing. Similarly, he is able to load Netscape and visit his favorite web sites (usually the Disney Store and Star Wars' sites) and browse the Web. Fortunately, he is too young to have accessed my credit card!

If all of these computer-based opportunities sound inviting but you do not have access to a computer at home or work—or if you do, and you just don't know how to start—ask for help from your local university, department of education, public or school library, or even the students in your class. Somebody will be happy to get you connected.

The Challenge of the Ever-Evolving Internet

As mentioned earlier in the discussion on searching ERIC on-line (see chapter 2), to conduct a review of related literature, it is important to note the changing nature of Internet-based resources. In all likelihood some of the "URL" addresses included here will have changed by the time you use them. However, if you learn to use your computer's search engine (for example, Yahoo, Lycos, and so on) you will be able to locate anything that is discussed here even if it has changed addresses. In many cases, going to the address provided results in a link or forwarding address to the new location, not dissimilar to the forwarding address provided by a post office when informed of a person's move to a new location. Simply update your "bookmark" so that you can return to the correct address quickly. Alternatively, you could visit my action research web site at http://beta.open.k12.or.us/~dennis/arowhelp/index.html for the current web site address.

Caution: Monitor Your Time On-Line

On-line time can be engaging, but expensive in terms of your time. This discussion of on-line resources is offered as an invitation to learn how to enhance your action research efforts, not as a way to devour your precious time. If you have access to the Internet and this virtual world is already commonplace for you, you have no doubt already learned to limit your time on the Web. On the other hand, if this all sounds troublesome and confusing, then it would be prudent to take one small step at a time. Maybe, with the assistance of your school's resident computer "hacker," you can investigate a few of the sites I have recommended in this chapter and find a few of your own. (Every school has a "hacker," or "CG" a.k.a. "computer guru." Ask around; you'll be surprised who it is! Even check with the students in your class, some of whom probably have their own web sites!) Whatever you do, don't let this journey into cyberspace eat up the time you have set aside for doing your action research. If you do, action research will quickly fall by the roadside to join other discarded educational innovations.

Caution: Be a Critical Consumer of On-Line Information

Perhaps this is stating the obvious (or re-stating it, since we briefly discussed this in chapters 2 and 7 as well), but do not assume that everything you read, see, and hear on-line has been subjected to any scrutiny by experts. What comes across your screen could be shared by just about anyone, anywhere, and without any consideration of accuracy. You will quickly gain a renewed interest in the concepts of validity and reliability when you read postings from all over the world. This does not mean that what you find on-line is garbage (I wonder if they call this "space junk" in cyberspace?!). Rather, be cautious about accepting anything that you find in this medium as "published" or "refereed" just because it appears on a computer monitor. Apply the same personal evaluative criteria you apply to anything you read, and your common sense will ensure good choices. Be a critical consumer of the information you find on-line.

Personal Reflection

All of this talk about cyberspace and virtual universities makes me think of my eighty-four-year-old dad again and what his reaction to all of this would be. I suspect that it would invoke a wry smile, a subtle turn of the head, and a remark such as, "You know, son, you just can't beat sitting down with your mates (Australian for *friends*) at the pub (Australian for a place to have a cold beverage) and having a good old chin wag (Australian for conversation)." Maybe the message from an elder of the tribe and the message for accessing on-line action research resources are essentially the same—use the medium to talk to your teacher researcher friends in the "virtual" cyberspace community and enjoy the interactions and learning that occurs. (I haven't resolved the "pub" part of the story but I am sure that cyberspace hackers are tackling such a pressing global problem at this very moment!)

Summary

The use of on-line action research resources can engage teacher researchers in discussion with like-minded teachers as part of a global learning community via the Internet. Web sites are valuable starting points for learning about what the Web has to offer. Listservs and on-line journals are also valuable resources that can further teacher researchers' understandings of current literature and the nature of theoretical and practical debates being undertaken by the wider action research community. Finally, become aware of the challenges posed by the Internet and the need to be cautious in allocating your time and assessing the information you find online.

For Further Thought

1. What on-line web site resources did you identify as most helpful for your work? Why?
2. Subscribe to a listserv. What did you learn? What did you contribute to the discussion?
3. Visit the on-line journal sources listed in this chapter. What steps do you need to follow to get your story published?
4. What problems did you face in using the on-line resources? How did you resolve the issues?
5. What advice would you have for colleagues about using the Internet?

CHAPTER 9

Action Research in Action: a Case Study of Curtis Elementary

This chapter includes a case study of Jonathan Stewart, a fifth-grade teacher at Curtis Elementary School. This account of Jonathan's study of the effects of an "altered curriculum" on student achievement in reading follows the framework for action research outlined in chapters 1 through 8 of this text. The case is offered not as an ideal for action research but rather as yet another example (this time, a more detailed one) of what action research looks like in practice. This case also illustrates how action research can be embedded into the culture of a Professional Development School (PDS) through cooperative work between public school and university faculty.

After reading this chapter you should be able to

1. Describe what good action research looks like in practice.
2. Apply the criteria for judging action research to the case study of Jonathan Stewart at Curtis Elementary school.
3. Discuss how you will represent your own action research projects.

The Setting: Curtis Elementary—A Professional Development School

Curtis Elementary is a small K through 5 urban elementary school with 256 children and twelve teachers. Located in the Pacific Northwest town of Cedarwood (population 18,000), Curtis Elementary was built in 1949. The limitations of the structure became evident when the school, like others in Cedarwood, received a grant to purchase computers for each classroom. The result—the school needed to be rewired to cope with the extra strain on the electrical system! The building is also considered to be "at risk" in the event of an earthquake and regularly undergoes structural inspections. A new wing was recently added to the school to house music and drama classes. The school also has an extensive playground that abounds with activity during the school day and a soccer/softball field that is used by community groups (such as the YMCA) for after-school sports.

For the most part, the teachers and principal have been working at the school for an average of ten years and all report high levels of satisfaction with the teaching/learning environment. Cedarwood Elementary boasts a high level of parental involvement in school activities and a supportive Parent-Teacher Association as well as a supportive community. This support manifests itself in regular school-sponsored field trips, materials to enhance the curriculum (in particular computer software), and teacher appreciation luncheons.

The demographics of the school are as follows: 256 students, 12 classroom teachers, and 10 certified support personnel. The ethnic background of the students is Native American (2%), Hispanic (4%), African American (5%), Asian (5%), and Caucasian (84%). All of the teachers are Caucasian, and most of them live in Cedarwood. Some of the teachers have children who attend the school. The general socioeconomic status of the community is revealed by the following statistic: twenty-seven percent (27%) of the students are eligible for "free or reduced lunch," making the school eligible for federal Chapter One funding.

The principal has been at the school for fifteen years and is highly respected by the teachers, children, and parents for his leadership of the school, particularly through an era of embedding technology in the school to improve teacher productivity and enhance curriculum. The principal is described by his teachers as being "caring, thoughtful, and an educational leader," and he facilitates many of the decisions affecting curriculum and instruction through a consensus, school-based decision-making process. The principal has also worked closely with faculty from the local university in areas of program development and student teacher selection and placement in public schools in the region.

Curtis Elementary is a **Professional Development School (PDS)**, or "partner" school with the local university. Professional Development Schools (analogous to teaching hospitals in the medical profession) are based on the following principles:

- **Reciprocity**—Mutual exchange and benefit between research and practice.
- **Experimentation**—Willingness to try new forms of practice and structure.
- **Systematic Inquiry**—The requirement that new ideas be subject to careful study and validation.

- **Student Diversity**—Commitment to the development of teaching strategies for a broad range of children with different backgrounds, abilities, and learning styles.

Professional Development Schools such as Curtis Elementary are "settings for teaching professionals to test different instructional arrangements, for novice teachers and researchers to work under the guidance of gifted practitioners, for the exchange of professional knowledge between university faculty and practitioners, and for the development of new structures designed around the demand of a new profession" (Holmes Group, 1986 p. 67). In PDSs, experienced teachers help teach and induct new members into the profession. In doing so, these experienced teachers also continue their quest to become better teachers themselves.

Curtis has used its PDS relationship with the university to drive school improvement efforts via action research. The partnership has created a synergistic relationship of public school teachers, preservice teachers, and university professors who can complement each other's skills. These are not research projects developed by professors to study teachers and children. They are collaborative, systematic, long-term efforts focused on improving teaching and learning. They are activities that can ultimately enhance the lives of children in classrooms. What follows is a description of the action research process as experienced by one teacher during a year at Curtis Elementary.

The Area of Focus: Constructing Meaning in Reading

The educators at Curtis Elementary have collectively agreed to make reading instruction a priority. As a team, they have decided that the general focus for action research efforts at Curtis Elementary will be on how children construct meaning in reading and how teachers can enhance student learning. After many collaborative discussions and reconnaissance activities, the members of the action research teams determined the school's area of focus would be: What is the effect of an "altered curriculum" on student performance? They defined an altered curriculum as an individual teacher's changes in what reading was taught and how it was taught based on professional development activities focused on constructing meaning in reading.

These decisions (and others like them) were based on reflective conversations like this one held at the weekly early morning faculty meetings at the beginning of the year:

Principal: As you know, I've been working for the past few weeks trial-running interview questions and strategies with students in grades 3, 4, and 5. From these interviews, it's clear that children use a variety of techniques for constructing meaning in their reading.

Teacher 1: One of the things I've been sitting here thinking about is the difference for our students between reading fiction and nonfiction.

Principal: I think that you're right. I wonder what this means for the way that we teach children to construct meaning in their reading.

Teacher 2: I read some research recently that indicated that children construct meaning by connecting what they are reading to other concepts they have learned.

Teacher 3: That's real similar to what happens in mathematics when children construct meaning. They link their new knowledge to existing knowledge.

FIGURE 9-1   Sources Provided by ERIC for Teachers at Curtis Elementary

Web Sites
- ERIC Clearinghouse on Reading, English, and Communication
  http://www.indiana.edu/~eric_rec
- Reading for Meaning
  http://www.sasked.gov.sk.ca/docs/ela_mean.html
- Vocabulary Instruction and Reading Comprehension
  http://www.indiana.edu/~eric_rec/ieo/digests/d126.html
- Reading Comprehension Instructional Strategies—Elementary Level
  http://www.indiana.edu/~eric_rec/ieo/bibs/rdcompel.html
- How to Improve Reading Comprehension
  http://www.marin.cc.ca.us/~don/Study/7read.html

Readings
- Barrentine, Shelby, et al. (1995). Reading mini-lessons: An instructional practice for meaning centered reading programs. Grand Forks, ND: Center for Teaching and Learning, University of North Dakota.
- Cote, Nathalie, et al. (1995). Children's use of prior knowledge and experience in making sense of informational text. Paper presented at the annual meeting of the American Educational Research Association, San Francisco, CA. April 18–22, 1995.
- Cothern, Nancy, B., et al. (1990). Using readers' imagery of literacy characters to study text meaning construction. *Reading Research and Instruction, 30* (1), 15–29.
- Dugan, JoAnn-Rubino, & Bean, Rita M. (1997). Side-by-side reading: Scaffolding meaning-making through literature discussions. Paper presented at the annual meeting of the American Educational Research Association, Chicago, IL. March 24–28, 1997.
- Hass, Christina, & Flower, Linda. (1988). Rhetorical reading strategies and the construction of meaning. *College Composition and Communication, 39* (2), 167–183.
- Keene, Ellin Oliver & Zimmermann, Susan. (1997). Mosaic of thought: Teaching comprehension in a reader's workshop. Portsmouth, NH: Heinemann.
- Kucer, Stephen, L. (1985). The making of meaning: Reading and writing, as parallel processes. *Written Communication, 2* (3), 317–336.
- Langer, Judith, A. (1986). Reading, writing, and understanding: An analysis of the construction of meaning. *Written Communication, 3* (2), 219–267.
- Mosenthal, Peter, B. (1987). Research views: Understanding meaning in reading. *Reading Teacher; 41* (2), 206–209.
- Oded, Brenda, & Stavans, Anat. (1994). The effect of "false" schema activation on the construction of meaning. *System, 22* (4), 497–507.
- Rowell, Jack, A., et al. (1990). The construction of meaning from text: Possible effects of different reading strategies. *Educational Psychology: An International Journal of Experimental Educational Psychology, 10* (1), 39–55.
- Tierney, Robert, J. (1990). Redefining reading comprehension. *Educational Leadership, 47* (6), 37–42.
- Wangberg, Elaine, G. (1983). Instructional strategies for implementing a reading for meaning approach. *Reading Horizons, 23* (4), 259–262.

Principal: Let me share with you one more story from a third grader. It appears as though she felt unable to trust her guesses about what was happening in the story, but she also gave me a vivid example of how she used visualization to construct meaning. I think that some of these examples point to how children use prior knowledge and context to construct meaning.

Teacher 4: It makes me think about how we create opportunities for students to create meaning in all of the different strategies I use in my classroom. But to be honest with you, while the information you have collected from the interviews with the students is so rich, I think that it's unrealistic to expect us to interview all of our students.

Principal: I think that you're right about that, which is why I think we should involve our preservice teachers in data collection. It will also satisfy a university course requirement for them. But I do think that these data are very rich and can help us understand how our students create meaning and what the effects of our reading strategies are on increasing their ability to construct meaning.

Reviewing the Literature

A subcommittee of the teachers conducted a review of literature. They consulted sources already present in the school: professional journals, teachers with advanced preparation in reading, and faculty from the university. They also accessed literature via the Internet through the AskERIC Service for educators and the AskERIC Q&A service (askeric@askeric.org). A list of sources provided by ERIC for teachers at Curtis Elementary is shown in Figure 9-1.

Creating an Action Plan

To guide them through their year-long action research projects, the teachers created action plans in conjunction with the principal. These action plans were used to guide and document the teachers' action research projects. Fifth-grade teacher Jonathan Stewart's action plan looked like this:

■■

Creating Meaning in Reading
JONATHAN STEWART

Area of Focus Statement

I am concerned about the ability of students in my classroom to construct meaning as they read. I teach fifth grade and feel that in my teaching of reading I have resorted more to emphasizing volume (the number of books children read) than to creating meaning (whether or not children really understand what they are reading). I guess that by the time children come to my fifth grade class I have started to take for granted that they already know how to read and how to create meaning from what they read. As last year's statewide assessment scores indicated, I (and other teachers in this school) need to challenge the assumption that older children have already developed the skills to read and create meaning by the fifth grade. Therefore, the purpose of this study is to describe the effect of an "altered curriculum" on student achievement in reading.

Defining the Variables

As a whole faculty we defined an altered curriculum as an individual teacher's changes in how reading was taught based on professional development activities focused on constructing meaning in reading. Student performance was defined as the scores children earned on statewide assessment tests and regularly administered teacher-made tests during the year.

Research Question

What is the effect of an altered curriculum on student performance?

Intervention

The reading intervention that I implement in my class will be developed on the basis of the professional development activities we engage in as a faculty. I anticipate that these activities will include a renewed emphasis on comprehension skills and diagnostic techniques and a greater understanding of exactly how children create meaning from what they read. I am also hoping that the literature will reveal some promising practices that I might consider for use in my classroom.

Membership of the Action Research Group

All of the teachers in the school have adopted the same action research goal for the year. However, we are working individually with the specific interventions that we feel are most appropriate for the students in our individual classrooms.

Negotiations to be Undertaken

The principal fully supports the action research process and will use individual teacher's documentation of the process and classroom observations of teaching as major components of the annual teacher evaluation cycle. I will need to negotiate my individual action research project with the principal, especially if I need to purchase any resources.

Timeline

Summer—Search ERIC for literature. Do professional reading. Attend professional development activities offered by the university. Take graduate class in reading.

Fall—Work with other teachers to determine appropriate professional development opportunities. Develop the specifics of my "creating meaning" reading intervention. Develop data collection strategies and collect some baseline data.

Winter–Spring—Implement intervention and collect data. Meet regularly with colleagues to discuss the effects of the intervention.

Spring—Analyze and interpret data and present findings to the faculty during an action research celebration. Plan the next cycle in the action research process.

Resources

- Paid non-contract time during summer to work on reviewing the literature.
- Support to attend summer institute on reading.
- Tuition reimbursement for cost of graduate credit.

Data Collection Ideas

- Interviews with students in my class.
- Observations during reading activities.
- Statewide assessment scores.
- Regular collection of student work.

Following the summer activities, Jonathan developed a formal data collection plan that included multiple-choice activities, cloze activities, and oral story telling activities, as outlined below.

Data Collection

During the school year I will use three different sources of data to help me "see" how my fifth graders are able to construct meaning when interacting with given passages of printed text. These data sources will include:

1. Multiple-choice, comprehension/recall activities using reading passages from grade levels 3 through 6.
2. Cloze procedures involving the students in the oral reading of a passage, at grade level, on Paul Bunyan, in which they will orally supply missing words from the text which complete the meaning of the passage.
3. Reading and retelling of a passage, at grade level, about the Bermuda Triangle (to name one example), in which the students will be allowed to read the passage as many times as they wish and to write/draw a retelling of the passage in their own words.

Data Analysis and Interpretation

Obviously, the only way I have of "knowing" that my students have reacted favorably to the curriculum and instruction changes used to implement my vocabulary focus on constructing meaning from the written work is to witness those students as they read, write, and interpret those same written words, both in context and individually. For the sake of brevity, I will simply share one situation that I have seen this year relating to each of the goals of increased vocabulary and meaning.

In the middle of a total group reading of "Thunder Cave" by Roland Smith, I was stopped by the class to recognize just how important it was that Jake, the young hero of the story, had been said to have handed a "folded" letter to a foreign official as part of a Visa request process. This carried great meaning to me in that they had to realize (construct meaning) that, since the letter was to have come from his father in Africa and that he had just forged the letter on his own computer only blocks away, the insight to fold the letter rather than just bring it in flat was absolutely necessary for the story to hold credibility to both the official and the reading audience. (*Note:* When my class brought this passage up to the author, who visited our school in person, he had to admit he had never thought about it in quite that much

detail, but he was glad that he had done it correctly by their critical standards of reading!)

During our annual Storytelling Unit this year, it was specifically brought to my mind by several of my twenty-five students, as they were "learning by heart" their tell-able tales, that some words used by the re-tellers of the chosen tales you just "had to memorize to use well" or the meaning of the story would change. As one student put it, "If they (the audience) can't understand that her venomous personality was snake-like, then I'll just have to add a line that lets them know that she really behaved like a snake and even looked like one at times." (*Note:* One student asked to be allowed to perform the same story she had done last year in fourth grade because she felt that this year she really understood what the story was about and could tell it in a more believable way.)

Student writings and rewritings show how they are constructing meaning either as a response to something they have already read or in thinking about how they want their readers to react to what they have put down on paper. For example, the following student dialogue evolved between a classmate and a peer proofreader and captures the essence of creating meaning:

> "Charlie, how badly is this guy supposed to be hurt in this part of the story?"
> "Not too bad. He's just got a cut on his forearm from the knife and it's bandaged up already."
> "Then don't you think that *gushed* is a little strong for the way the blood was coming out of the bandage? Maybe it should be *ooze* or *seep*?

When the children are having the discussions, asking the questions, and making the clarifying statements with each other, the teaching is invisible and at its highest level. Words weave wondrous webs!

Of the various factors of meaning construction I observed through the use of the data collection techniques, the most striking to me was the pivotal importance of each student "knowing or not knowing" the meaning of the vocabulary used in the story—not just the words "at grade level" that are the basic glue for the verbal presentation, but rather the "extended or specialized" terms that truly gave personality, character, and depth to the writing. Especially through the cloze procedure I was able to witness, with my own ears, the mental processing that some readers could, and others could not, employ to generate a meaningful and appropriate word choice to continue, complete, and in many cases, enrich a pre-initiated idea.

I was most aware of my students' reactions to and use of heightened vocabulary to increase their construction of meaning through three different activities:

1. Students recognize through a word replacement activity that it is very difficult to maintain the meaning of a well-written passage or sentence if you are trying to replace certain specifically selected words in that segment.
2. Students have "voiced" the feelings and mental pictures brought forth in their minds by different passages, both read and listened to, during various curricular reading assignments.
3. Student writing samples demonstrate how well they absorb and use different writing styles, voice, and word selection to create a more interesting, engaging, and detailed piece of writing.

The Findings

Based on my data analysis and interpretation, I will present the following findings of my study of the effects of an altered curriculum on student achievement to the other teachers and the principal:

- A high level of the skills and knowledge developed in professional development settings transferred to my classroom practice.
- Students understand the difficult nature of word replacement in activities where they try to replace words and maintain the meaning of a passage.
- As students have learned to create meaning during reading, they can discuss the feelings and mental pictures evoked by the passage.
- Students' ability to create meaning of what they read is also evident in their abilities to create interesting, engaging, and detailed writing of their own.

Action Planning

Though I have long been a person who loves to play with words and understands their massive power, I have never really tried to pass on that idea of literal word power. I plan to continue to emphasize looking for, reading, discussing, understanding, and employing the added power that well-used vocabulary can create in both oral and written expression.

My focus on vocabulary reinforcement will be extended through the following areas of reading and written expression with my students: group novels, published poetry, current events magazines, storytelling collections, student-created stories, narratives, opinion papers, descriptions, research papers, and oral presentations.

I plan to use the following in-class techniques to monitor, modify, and evaluate the impact and effectiveness of my vocabulary intensification efforts: observations of student learning, reflections with students (oral, written, individual, and group), and continued assessment using the data-gathering techniques mentioned earlier (multiple-choice activities, cloze activities, and oral storytelling activities). Students will also make regular journal entries recording their own observations of how different wording has affected their construction of meaning.

I have already implemented several teaching and curriculum changes as a result of this action research project. One helpful technique was my asking students to look up certain vocabulary words from selected novel selections, to know the meaning of the word as it was used in the section, and then to try to replace the word with another word or phrase that maintained the flow and intent of the chosen sentence. Students are already finding out why the author chose a particular word for the intent of the sentence.

I am sure that as I start the next cycle of action research I will be "constructing meaning" of my

TABLE 9-1 Jonathan Stewart's Steps to Action Chart

Summary of Findings Research Questions	Recommended Action Targeted to Findings	Who Is Responsible for the Action? T - Teacher S - Student P- Principal PA - Parents	Who Needs to Be Consulted or Informed?	Who Will Monitor/ Collect Data	Timeline	Resources
1.0 What is the effect of an altered curriculum on student performance?					Ongoing throughout school year.	
1.1 High level of transfer of P.D. skills and knowledge to classroom practice.	1.1 Continue to monitor transfer of P.D. skills and to modify and evaluate vocabulary intensification efforts.	1.1 T	1.1 T, P	1.1–1.4 Multiple-choice activities. Cloze procedures.		1.1 $'s for P.D. and tuition reimbursement.
1.2 Students' understanding of word replacement strategies was high.	1.2–1.4 Continue to implement strategies that improve students' abilities to create meaning in their reading and writing.	1.2–1.4 T, S	1.2–1.4 T, P, S, Pa	Retelling passage/story activities.		1.2–1.4 $'s for curriculum materials.
1.3 Students were able to create meaning during reading and to discuss feelings and mental pictures.				Student journal writing.		
1.4 Students were able to create meaning through their own writing.						

own about how children construct meaning. The constant inquisitive nature of my fifth-grade learners will ensure that we are continually thinking together about our reading and how to improve ourselves.

On-Line Resources

Throughout the year, I visited the following on-line sites to research the literature, check for promising practices and current trends within the professional organizations in the area of reading, and discuss my action research work-in-progress with other teachers across the nation:

- ERIC—I used the AskERIC Q&A service to conduct an electronic search of the literature related to my area of focus.

- Association for Supervision and Curriculum Development (http://odie.ascd.org).
- International Reading Association (http://www.ira.org)—The IRA offers grants to support teacher research (up to $5,000) through their Teacher as Researcher Grants. I also discovered that the IRA homepage had links to their Research and Policy Division and links to upcoming research conferences and meetings.
- PARnet—I visited the PARnet website (http://www.parnet.org) to see if any other teachers were working on similar action research projects.
- Arlist—I subscribed to the action research listserv and monitored conversations.

Sharing the Findings

The faculty at Cedarwood Elementary met once a month for regular professional development activities related to the "creating meaning in reading" area of focus. Most of these activities were held after school and culminated with a dinner discussion at a restaurant or faculty member's house. These forums for discourse are embedded in the culture of Cedarwood Elementary and are funded by the school's professional development fund.

Critiquing Action Research

Now, let's take a few moments to apply the criteria for judging action research (from chapter 7) to Jonathan Stewart's action research project. Before proceeding with this activity, take a few minutes to write down your reactions to the study and whether you think that it is "good" action research.

Audience

Who was the intended audience for the action research report? Jonathan's report was intended primarily for himself and his principal, but it found a wider audience with other teachers at Curtis Elementary. With this audience in mind it would appear as though Jonathan's report satisfies these criteria. The principal was satisfied with the detail included in Jonathan's report and felt that it provided him with another "window" into Jonathan's teaching practices and his ability to make curriculum and instruction changes on the basis of data.

Format

Was the report presented using an acceptable format? All teachers' reports of their action research projects at Curtis Elementary were shared using the same format— a brief written report using these headings: area of focus, review of literature, action plan, data collection, data analysis and interpretation, steps to action, and on-line resources. This faculty had collaboratively determined that this was an acceptable format for sharing their action research inquiries with their colleagues and the principal.

Prejudices

Are there any prejudices that might affect the findings of the study? Jonathan does not explicitly state any prejudices he may have had regarding the area of focus. There is no indication of whether or not Jonathan had preconceived notions about the outcomes or conduct of the study.

Professional Disposition

How has the action research effort contributed to the teacher's professional disposition? This is perhaps best summed up in Jonathan's words when he says, "I am sure that as I start the next cycle of action research I will be 'constructing meaning' of my own about how students construct meaning. The constant inquisitive nature of my fifth-grade learners will ensure that we are continually thinking together about our reading and how to improve ourselves." This statement appears to capture the spirit of a professional disposition of a teacher who is committed to being a lifelong learner and willing to make changes if needed.

Reflective Stance

In what ways has the action research effort contributed to Jonathan's reflective stance and how he views teaching and learning? Jonathan's professional disposition now appears to embrace a reflective stance and show a willingness to continue with the action research process to monitor the impact of his intervention during the next year.

Life Enhancing

Have Jonathan's efforts enhanced the lives of the children in his care? It appears from Jonathan's narrative and examples of the children's voices that the ability to read and write, with an increased understanding of the meaning of the text, has been enhanced.

Action

What action did Jonathan take based on his findings? Jonathan implemented a reading curriculum that enhanced vocabulary development through reading and written expression activities involving group novels, published poetry, current events magazines, storytelling collections, student-created stories, narratives, opinion papers, descriptions, research papers, and oral presentations. Students also incorporated regular journal entries recording their own observations of how different wording has affected their construction of meaning.

Action-Data Connection

How is Jonathan's proposed action connected to his data analysis and interpretation? Jonathan's narrative includes some references to data that informed his decision making, including observations of students as they read, write, and interpret written words in context; multiple-choice comprehension/recall activities; cloze procedures involving oral reading tasks; and writing, drawing, and retelling passages from stories. The data presented in Jonathan's case suggest a strong action-data connection. That is, Jonathan's proposed actions are connected to the data he collected, analyzed, and interpreted.

Impact

How will Jonathan continue to monitor the effects of his practice? Jonathan will continue to monitor his "altered curriculum" to enhance student construction of meaning in reading by using many of the same data collection techniques he incorporated into his first action research cycle.

Changes

What will Jonathan do differently during the next action research cycle? Jonathan will continue with his reading intervention as it was originally developed, but he is open to incorporating any new promising practices that emerge from his continued professional development opportunities. Jonathan will also add to his data collection strategies the use of journal writings in which students reflect on how they create meaning in reading.

Colleague Response

How did Jonathan's colleagues respond to the actions recommended by his research? Jonathan, like the other teachers at Curtis Elementary School, presented developments in his action research project throughout the school year. This ongoing discourse about what was being learned during the study is not captured in Jonathan's narrative, but is a regular part of life at Curtis Elementary. Jonathan's account could have included more information about how colleagues responded to his research and how it compared to the findings of other teachers who worked on the same area of focus.

Celebrating Action Research

At the end of the school year, the faculty at Curtis Elementary participated in an "Action Research Fair," during which the learning community celebrated their individual and collective insights about the impact of their "creating meaning in reading" interventions on student achievement. This event provided an opportunity for the teachers, preservice teachers, and university faculty to celebrate the action research process and to recommit to another year of professional development and goal setting.

Final Thoughts

We have now been through the full cycle of the action research process. We have read about the historical antecedents and theories that underpin action research. We have read about (and ideally, put into practice) each of the four steps in the process. We have read action research vignettes that breathe life into the process and demystify what action research might look like in practice. We are now ready to move on to the next action research cycle.

Action research is a process, but it is also a way of thinking and being. Becoming a teacher researcher means making a commitment to continually reflect on the way things are in our classrooms and schools and striving to learn what we can do to make them better. Your decision to do action research—your commitment to this way of thinking and being—contributes to the revitalization of the teaching profession. Your willingness to embark on this intimate, open-ended, creative journey called action research will be rewarded with the knowledge that our students are the benefactors of our search for excellence in education.

Summary

This chapter provided a case study of Jonathan Stewart, a fifth-grade teacher at Curtis Elementary School. This case study captured much of what Jonathan did during his study of the effects of an "altered curriculum" on student achievement in reading. This case also exemplified how action research can be embedded into the culture of a Professional Development School (PDS) through cooperative work between public school and university faculty.

For Further Thought

1. What did you learn from Jonathan Stewart's case study that can help with your own action research?
2. How would you apply the criteria for judging the quality of action research to Jonathan Stewart's case?
3. How can you develop a collaborative action research network that involves your school's principal and teachers with other educators (such as preservice teachers, university faculty, and so on)?

References

Adelman, C. (1993). Kurt Lewin and the origins of action research. *Educational Action Researcher, 1*(1), 7–25.

Agar, M. H. (1980). *The professional stranger: An informal introduction to ethnography.* Orlando, FL: Academic Press.

Anderson, G. L., Herr, K., & Nihlen, A. S. (1994). *Studying your own school: An educator's guide to qualitative practitioner research.* Thousand Oaks, CA: Corwin Press.

Anderson, L. W., & Burns, R. B. (1989). *Research in classrooms: The study of teachers, teaching and instruction.* New York: Pergamon Press.

Calhoun, E. F. (1994). *How to use action research in the self-renewing school.* Alexandria, VA: ASCD.

Cochran-Smith, M., & Lytle, S. L. (1993). *Inside outside: Teacher research and knowledge.* New York: Teachers College Press.

Conley, S. (1991). Review of research on teacher participation in school decision making. *Review of Research in Education, 17,* 225–266.

Cronbach, L. J., & Meehl, P. E. (1955). Construct validity in psychological tests. *Psychological Bulletin, 52*(4), 281–302.

Cunningham, J. B. (1983). Gathering data in a changing organization. *Human Relations, 36*(5) 403–420.

Deal, T. (1987). The culture of schools. In Sheive, L. T. & Schoenheit, M. B. (Eds.), *Leadership: Examining the elusive* (pp. 3–15). Alexandria, VA: ASCD.

Denzin, N. (1997). *Interpretive ethnography.* Thousand Oaks, CA: Sage.

Eisenhart, M. A., & Howe, K. R. (1992). Validity in educational research. *In* M. D. LeCompte, W. L. Millroy, & J. Preissle (Eds.), *The Handbook of Qualitative Research in Education* (pp. 643–680). San Diego, CA: Academic Press.

Eisner, E. W. (1991). *The enlightened eye: Qualitative inquiry and the enhancement of educational practice.* New York: Macmillan.

Elliott, J. (1991). *Action research for educational change.* Bristol, PA: Open University Press.

Flinders, D. J. (1992). In search of ethical guidance: Constructing a basis for dialogue. *Qualitative Studies in Education, 5*(2), 101–115.

Foucault, M. (1972). *The archaeology of knowledge.* New York: Random House.

Fueyo, V., & Koorland, M. A. (1997). Teacher as researcher: A synonym for professionalism. *Journal of Teacher Education, 48* (5), 336–344.

Fullan, M. (1997). Emotion and hope: Constructive concepts for complex times. In A. Hargreaves (Ed.), *Rethinking educational change with heart and mind.* (pp. 216–233). Alexandria, VA: ASCD.

Fullan, M. (1993). *Change forces: Probing the depths of educational reform.* New York: The Falmer Press.

Fullan, M. (1985). Change processes and strategies at the local level. *Elementary School Journal, 85* (3), 391–421.

Fullan, M. (1982). *The meaning of educational change.* New York: Teachers College Press.

Gay, L. R. (1996). *Educational research: Competencies for analysis and application.* Upper Saddle River, NJ: Merrill/Prentice Hall.

Grundy, S. (1994). Action research at the school level: Possibilities and problems. *Educational Action Research, 2*(1), 23–36.

Guba, E. G. (1981). Criteria for assessing the trustworthiness of naturalistic inquiries. *Educational Communication and Technology, 29*(2), 75–91.

Gunz, J. (1996). Jacob L. Moreno and the origins of action research. *Educational Action Research, 4*(1), 145–148.

Hammersley, M. (1993). On the teacher as researcher. *Educational Action Research, 1*(3), 425–441.

Hitchcock, G., & Hughes, D. (1989). *Research and the teacher: A qualitative introduction to school-based research.* New York: Routledge.

Holmes Group. (1995). *Tomorrow's schools of education.* East Lansing, MI: The Holmes Group.

Holmes Group. (1990). *Tomorrow's schools.* East Lansing, MI: The Holmes Group.

Holmes Group. (1986). *Tomorrow's teachers.* East Lansing, MI: The Holmes Group.

Hord, S., Rutherford, W. L., Huling-Austin, L., & Hall, G. E. (1987). *Taking charge of change.* Alexandria, VA: ASCD.

Jackson, P. (1968). *Life in classrooms.* New York: Holt, Rinehart, & Winston.

Jennings, L. E., & Graham, A. P. (1996). Postmodern perspectives and action research: Reflecting on the possibilities. *Educational Action Research, 4*(2), 267–278.

Joyce, B. R., Hersh, R. H., & McKibben, M. (1983). *The structure of school improvement.* New York: Longman.

Kemmis, S. (1982). Action research in retrospect and prospect. In S. Kemmis & R. McTaggart (Eds.), *The action research reader.* Geelong, Vic: Deakin University Press.

Kemmis, S., & McTaggart, R. (Eds.). (1988a). *The action research reader* (3rd ed.). Geelong, Victoria, Australia: Deakin University Press.

Keemis, S., & McTaggert, R. (Eds.). (1988b). *The action research planner* (3rd ed.). Geelong, Victoria, Australia: Deakin University Press.

Kennedy, Mary M. (1997) The connection between research and practice. *Educational Researcher, 26* (7), 4–12.

Kincheloe, J. (1991). Teachers as researchers: Qualitative inquiry as a path to empowerment. Philadelphia: Falmer Press.

Lewin, K. (1952). Group decision and social change. In G. E. Swanson, T. M. Newcomb, & E. L. Hartley (Eds.). *Readings in Social Psychology.* New York: Henry Holt.

Lewin, K. (1946). Action research and minority problems. *Journal of Social Issues, 2,* 34–46.

Lieberman, A. (1988). Teachers and principals: Turf, tension, and new tasks. *Phi Delta Kappan,* May, 648–653.

Lortie, D. C. (1975). *Schoolteacher.* Chicago: The University of Chicago Press.

Lytle, S. (1997). Action research keynote address. Kansas City, MO: The Learning Exchange.

McMillan, James H. (1996). Educational research: Fundamentals for the consumer (2nd ed.). New York: Harper Collins College Publishers.

Maxwell, J. A. (1992). Understanding and validity in qualitative research. *Harvard Educational Review, 62*(3), 279–300.

Miller, L., & Lieberman, A. (1988). School Improvement in the United States: Nuance and numbers. *International Journal of Qualitative Studies in Education, 1*(1), 3–19.

Mills, G. E. (1997). *Action research and goals 2000: The Oregon story.* Paper presented at the 18th Annual Ethnography in Education Forum, University of Pennsylvannia, PA.

Mills, G. E. (1993). Levels of abstraction in a case study of educational change *In* D. J. Flinders & G. E. Mills (Eds.), *Theory and concepts in qualitative research: Perspectives from the field.* New York: Teachers College Press.

Mills, G. E. (1990). *A consumers' guide to school improvement.* Eugene, OR: ERIC Clearinghouse on Educational Management.

Mills, G. E. (1988). *Managing and coping with multiple educational change: A case study and analysis.* Unpublished doctoral dissertation. Eugene, OR: University of Oregon.

Mills, G. E. (1985). Transient children. Unpublished M.Ed. Thesis. Perth, Australia: Western Australian Institute of Technology.

National Council of Teachers of Mathematics. (1991). *Professional standards for teaching mathematics.* Reston, VA: National Council of Teachers of Mathematics.

Noffke, S. (1994). Action research: Towards the next generation. *Educational Action Research, 2*(1), 9–18.

Oja, N. S., & Smulyan, L. (1989). *Collaborative action research: A developmental approach.* Philadelphia, PA: Falmer Press.

Osterman, K. F., & Kottkamp, R. B. (1993). *Reflective practice for educators: Improving schooling through professional development.* Newbury Park, CA: Corwin Press.

Pelto, P. J., & Pelto, G. H. (1978). *Anthropological research: The structure of inquiry.* Cambridge, MA: Cambridge University Press.

Sagor, R. (1992). *How to conduct collaborative action research.* Alexandria, VA: ASCD.

Sarason, S. B., (1990). *The predictable failure of educational reform: Can we change course before it's too late?* San Francisco, CA: Jossey-Bass.

Sarason, S. B. (1982). *The culture of the school and the problem of change* (2nd ed.). Boston: Allyn & Bacon.

Sergiovanni, T. (1992). Why we should seek substitutes for leadership. *Educational Leadership, 49*(5), 41–45.

Smith, L. M. (1990). Ethics in qualitative field research: An individual perspective. In E. W. Eisner & A. P. Peshkin (Eds.), *Qualitative inquiry in education: The continuing debate.* New York: Teachers College Press.

Soltis, J. (1990). The ethics of qualitative research. In E. W. Eisner & A. P. Peshkin (Eds.), *Qualitative inquiry in education: The continuing debate.* New York: Teachers College Press.

Spradley, J. (1980). *Participant observation.* New York: Holt, Rinehart & Winston.

Stringer, E. T. (1996). *Action research: A handbook for practitioners.* Thousand Oaks, CA: Sage.

Stringer, E. T. (1993). Socially responsive educational research: Linking theory and practice. In D. Flinders, & G. E. Mills (Eds.), *Theory and concepts in qualitative research: Perspectives from the field* (pp. 141–162). New York: Teachers College Press.

Tickle, L. (1993). Testing for quality in educational action research: A terrifying taxonomy? *Educational Action Research, 3*(2), 233–236.

Tuckman, B. W. (1999). *Conducting educational research* (5th ed.). New York: Harcourt Brace.

Van De Walle, J. A. (1994). *Elementary school mathematics: Teaching developmentally.* New York: Longman.

Vockell, E. L., & Asher, J. W. (1996). *Educational research.* Upper Saddle River, NJ: Merrill/Prentice Hall.

Wells, G. (Ed.). (1994). *Changing schools from within: Creating communities of inquiry.* Portsmouth, NH: Heinemann.

Witte, R. S. (1985). *Statistics.* New York: Holt, Rinehart & Winston.

Wolcott, H. F. (1997). Ethnographic research in education. In *Complementary methods for research in education* (2nd ed.) (pp. 325–398). Washington, DC: American Educational Research Association.

Wolcott, H. F. (1995). *The art of fieldwork.* Walnut Creek, CA: AltaMira Press.

Wolcott, H. F. (1994). *Transforming qualitative data: Description, analysis, and interpretation.* Thousand Oaks, CA: Sage.

Wolcott, H. F. (1992). Posturing in qualitative inquiry. In M. LeCompte, W. L. Millroy, J. Preissle (Eds.), *Handbook of qualitative research in education* (pp. 3–52). San Diego, CA: Academic Press.

Wolcott, H. F. (1990). On seeking—and rejecting—validity in qualitative research. In E. W. Eisner & A. Peshkin (Eds.), *Qualitative inquiry in education: The continuing debate* (pp. 121–152). New York: Teachers College Press.

Wolcott, H. F. (1989). *Kwakiutl village and school.* Prospect Heights, IL: Waveland Press.

Wolcott, H. F. (1988). Ethnographic research in education. In R. M. Jaeger (Ed.), *Complementary methods for research in education* (pp. 187–210). Washington, DC: American Educational Research Association.

Wolcott, H. F. (1982). Differing styles of on-site research, or "If it isn't ethnography, what is it?" *Review Journal of Philosophy and Social Science, 7,* 154–169.

Wolcott, H. F. (1974). The elementary school principal: Notes from a field study. In G. Spindler (Ed.), *Education and cultural process: Toward an anthropology of education* (pp. 176–204). New York: Holt, Rinehart & Winston.

Index